PRAISE

MW00474362

"Your book made me laugh, cry, reflect, remember, and most of all, realize that I have BROTHERS who understand who no one else around me can fathom. It is great to be able to write and know they know."
-Hank Dunn, 2nd Battalion, 7th Cavalry on Landing Zone Albany

"I want to thank you for having the courage and God-given ability to put your emotions into words. I'm sure it was very difficult for you to do so, but it may have been a catharsis. It was the most powerful narrative of an individual combat soldier's conscience, heart, and psyche that I have ever heard."
-Vern Miller, Vietnam combat veteran.

"You put into words the thoughts that have been going through my mind for many years."
-Dick Ackerman, enlisted man, Co. D, 2nd Battalion, 7th Cavalry, on Landing Zone Albany

"...I couldn't put it down until I had read the entire book. Your words expressed exactly my feelings and those of many others of 2/7th I have spoken with."
-Sergeant Major James A. Scott, HQ Co., 2nd Battalion, 7th Cavalry, on Landing Zone Albany

"...It touched my heart."
-George Forrest, Captain and Company Commander, Co. A, 1st Battalion, 5th Cavalry, on Landing Zone Albany

"...I thought it was great—no, wonderful...It truly touched me, and for that I thank you."
-Bob Towles, enlisted man, Co. D, 2nd Battalion, 7th Cavalry, on Landing Zone Albany

"…It is so beautifully done and says so much so well—the truth has its own way of coming out so honestly and clear—there is no one who could have done this so well—I am so proud of you and your courage to do this."
-J.L. "Bud" Alley, Lieutenant, HQ Co.,
2nd Battalion, 7th Cavalry, on Landing Zone Albany

"…It is as powerful a piece on the brotherhood of war, the emotions of men surrounded by death and dying in combat, and the physical and emotional scars wars leave, as I have ever read."
-Doug Sams, Vietnam combat veteran

"I read… with heart in my throat. It is eerie, the unspoken but similar thoughts of Vietnam warriors. Many of your 'reflections' I understand, many I cannot even imagine. Thank you for your service, your blood, your devotion to country. Welcome Home."
-Jim Balkcom, Civilian Aide to the Secretary of the Army,
Atlanta, GA

REFLECTIONS ON LZ ALBANY
THE AGONY OF VIETNAM

To Matt —

I appreciate your
interest in American
military history.
I hope my writings
speak to you.

Jim Lawrence

REFLECTIONS ON LZ ALBANY

THE AGONY OF VIETNAM

JAMES T. LAWRENCE

DEEDS PUBLISHING | ATLANTA

Published by Deeds Publishing
Marietta, GA
www.deedspublishing.com

Printed in The United States of America

Library of Congress Cataloging-in-Publications Data is available upon request.

ISBN 978-1-937565-86-2

Books are available in quantity for promotional or premium use. For information, write Deeds Publishing, PO Box 682212, Marietta, GA 30068 or info@deedspublishing.com.

First Edition, 2014

10 9 8 7 6 5 4 3 2 1

CONTENTS

Acknowledgments   9
Introduction   15
A Special Dedication   17

The Band Of Brothers   23
Airborne   29
A. P. O. San Francisco   41
Conversations With A Tombstone   45
A Voice From The Wall   55
The Man And The Deer   59
The Mother   61
The Stare   65
The Premonition   71
Bringing In The Hueys   79
Did You Know, Mama?   93
The Gold Star Kid   97
Just Don't Ask Me   105
It's All Over   109
Dear John   117
She's Out There   123
The Valley Of The Shadow Of Death   127
Fields Of Fire   135
LZ Albany   143
History Repeated? An Opinion   163
About The Author   169

APPENDIX   **173**

The Men Of The Seventh   177
Come On Boys, Ride With Me   178
Victor Charlie   180
The Legend Of The Seventh Cavalry   181
Garryowen   184
Garryowen (7th Cavalry version)   186
Fiddler's Green   188

ACKNOWLEDGMENTS

THE THOUGHTS AND MEMORIES THAT make up these writings have been in my head for almost 50 years, and they would have remained there had it not been for the encouragement of many people. These friends talked to me, listened to me, empathized with me, encouraged me, and, in some cases, pushed me to pen these words and tell the stories of the brave men of the 2nd Battalion, 7th Cavalry who participated in the battle on Landing Zone Albany, and of the pains and sufferings of the families and friends of those men. To these, I say "thank you," because this book would not exist without your encouragements.

To Joe Griffin, my childhood friend in Troy, Alabama, a patriotic American and an outstanding preacher in St. Louis, Missouri, who remained a friend, a confidant, and invited me to speak to his congregation a few years back, which event confirmed that my story had value to Americans everywhere.

To my Birmingham, Alabama, real estate friends—Dot Mash, Mac Fairley, and Ty Dodge (himself a wounded Vietnam veteran)—who encouraged me and, in some cases, pushed me and pushed me hard to put my words on paper and to share my reflections of the story of Landing Zone Albany.

To Lt. General Hal Moore, the great combat leader of the 1st Battalion, 7th Cavalry, who directed his "troopers" in the furious two and one-half day battle on Landing Zone X-Ray on November 14—16, 1965, the other battle of the Ia Drang, and who showed me in later years the necessity and quality of leadership that is always needed to keep America great.

To Joe Galloway, the young UPI correspondent who rode a Huey into the Ia Drang and into history, the only civilian to be awarded the Bronze Star in the Vietnam War, and the author of many outstanding works, including co-authoring the two great pieces about our battle—*We Were Soldiers Once . . . and Young* and *We Are Soldiers Still*—for remaining a friend all these years and giving me encouragement and advice on the writing and printing of this work.

To Dr. Philip Beidler, a professor of English at the University of Alabama, a Vietnam veteran, and author of many acclaimed books including *Late Thoughts on an Old War: The Legacy of Vietnam*, for writing a very candid, accurate article in the Spring 2003 issue of *Alabama Heritage* periodical entitled "The Lost Battalion of the Ia Drang," confirming for me that we, the men of the 2nd Battalion, 7th Cavalry, had a story worth telling.

To Myra MacPherson, who was a political writer for The Washington Post and the author of the 1984 book, *Long Time Passing: Vietnam and The Haunted Generation,* who interviewed me for that book and made me realize that we, the Vietnam Vets, all carried a burden with which we must deal.

To Chris Cannon, an outstanding high school teacher in St. George, Utah, whom I met as a boatmen on a raft down the Colorado River through the Grand Canyon, who brought me to Utah and had me speak to two large groups of high school students, which confirmed that Americans needed and wanted to hear about the brave men of the 2nd Battalion, 7th Cavalry in combat.

To the members of the Fire Department of New York City, especially my friend Gerard Siani, who brought a steel beam from the World Trade Towers to Fort Benning, Georgia, on September 17, 2007, to honor the memory of Rick Rescorla, one of the heroes of the battle in the Ia Drang and of the attacks of 9/11, and celebrated with us, the veterans of the Battle of the Ia Drang Valley, reminding me that battles defending our freedoms can be fought in the highland jungles of Vietnam or the streets of New York City.

To Courtney Haden of Boutwell Studios in Homewood, Alabama, who spent hours with me in the recording of my writings onto compact discs and who wrote about us in Birmingham magazine, for finding value in our story.

To the memory of the 2nd Battalion, 7th Cavalry officer "warriors" of the Battle in the Ia Drang Valley—Major Frank Henry, Captain Myron Diduryk, Captain Jim Spires, Lieutenant John "Doc" Howard, Lieutenant Mike Kalla, and Lieutenant Rick Rescorla—who are my heroes and whose contributions on the battlefield must never, ever be forgotten.

To the officers of the 2nd Battalion, 7th Cavalry, Vietnam—especially Larry Gwin, Bud Alley, Hank Dunn, Pat Payne, Jim Lane, George Johnson, Joel Sugdinis, Enrique Pujals, Bob Jeanette, "Doc" Shucart, Jim Kelley, Bill McClure—whose fellowship and friendship continued to inspire me to write.

To the non-commissioned officers and the enlisted men of the 2nd Battalion, 7th Cavalry, Vietnam—especially Ron Benton, Donald Slovak, Bob Towles, Dick Ackerman, Russell Wilson, Bob Jones, Sam Fantino—whose presence at gatherings and reunions reminded me that we still had a story to tell.

To Pat Gartland, successful businessman in Marietta, Georgia, who invited me to speak to the Atlanta Vietnam Veterans Business Association and who put me in touch with Bob Babcock, the publisher of this book.

To the owners and staff of Deeds Publishing, LLC, of Marietta, Georgia—Bob Babcock, CEO, Jan Babcock, President, and Mark Babcock, Creative Director—for their professionalism, encouragement, and many hours of hard work, to ensure that my writings and our story finally became a reality, and allowed me to realize a lifetime goal of publishing this book.

To Sarah Lawrence, my mother, and Ann Lawrence Ballenger, my sister, who have always supported me and encouraged me.

To Kathy Lawrence, my wife, and Talbot Lawrence, my son, who supported, encouraged, and, often times, tolerated me while I wrestled with my "ghosts" of the Vietnam experience.

And, finally, to Madelyn Grace Lawrence, my grandchild, born on April 8, 2012, whose youthful presence made me continue to realized that every generation will perhaps require young Americans to fight for, and possibly die for, the tremendous values and freedoms that we, as Americans, must preserve and defend, and that those like me who have experienced combat have an obligation to communicate the necessity and yet horrific consequences of war.

INTRODUCTION

TO THE UNINITIATED, ALBANY IS the capital of New York State or a city in Georgia; to a very select few, Albany is a clearing in western Vietnam, just a short distance from the Cambodian border, where, on November 17, 1965, those few experienced a true hell on earth that has affected them every day since then.

On that day, the Second Battalion, Seventh Cavalry, First Cavalry Division (Airmobile) was ambushed by a larger fighting force of regular North Vietnamese soldiers. The Americans suffered 151 killed and 125 wounded but inflicted much greater losses on the enemy.

I was one of those Americans. I was a twenty-four-year-old first lieutenant, the executive officer of Delta Company, which was one of the companies overrun by the enemy. I suffered a physical wound that day and have lived with the mental and psychological scars of that battle ever since.

I write these lines to show, as best I can, the pains of war to all those blessed enough never to have experienced it. Ask any soldier who was there; they do not talk about medals, victory, and glory. They talk about individuals, hurts, horrors, and losses.

To those men who fought bravely, to those men who were wounded and survived, to those families who lost one they loved, and to those gallant men who gave their lives for their brothers and their country on that day in November of 1965, these lines are dedicated. And to my mother, Sarah Talbot Lawrence, who suffered through all of this.

James T. Lawrence
05 321 340

A SPECIAL DEDICATION

I WRITE THESE WORDS TO honor the memory of Lieutenant Donald Charles Cornett of Lake Charles, Louisiana. Born in Hazard, Kentucky, Don was the oldest child of Lt. Colonel Buster and Velma Cornett and the brother to sisters Carol and Peggy. He and his family moved to Lake Charles from Florida, where he began his junior year in college at McNeese State University. In only two years at McNeese, he earned many honors, including ROTC Cadet Commander, President of Scabbard and Blade, Who's Who in American Colleges and Universities, and was elected to Student Body President after only one year at McNeese.

During that time, he met and married the beautiful Sylvia Wright, on June 8, 1963, and together they welcomed their only child, Kevin Charles Cornett, born on November 9, 1964, after Don had received his commission into the United State Army and was stationed at Ft. Benning, Georgia. He entered the Army as a second lieutenant and was assigned to the 2nd Battalion, 9th Infantry, of the 2nd Infantry Division. He completed both

Airborne School and Ranger School while at Benning.

When the 2nd Infantry Division and the 11th Air Assault became the 1st Cavalry Division (Airmobile), Lt. Cornett became a platoon leader for Charlie Company, 2nd Battalion, 7th Cavalry, of the 1st Cav. Just weeks before the Ia Drang Vally campaign, he was promoted to first lieutenant and was named Executive Officer to the same Charlie Company. He was killed in the savage action on and around Landing Zone Albany on November, 17, 1965.

Don Cornett was, and still is, one of the finest men I have ever known, and, to this day, one of the best friends I have ever had. We were roommates in the Infantry Officer Basic Course, roommates in the barracks at Lawson Field for Airborne School, roommates on the troop ship, the USNS Maurice Rose, going to Vietnam, and greatest of friends until his untimely death.

Don represents the real tragedy of any war. There is no telling what this man would have accomplished had he lived. One way to gauge his potential greatness is to measure the reaction to him when his name comes up with the other lieutenants from that time of the 2nd of the 7th Cav. Each one of us refers to Don as "our best friend in the military." He had that uncanny ability of both leadership and friendship to cause all of us lieutenants to claim him as "best friend." He was that outstanding, that unique, that special.

I have written about him. He is the prototype for the buried soldier in "Conversations with a Tombstone," he is the "Voice from the Wall" in the piece by that same name, he is the more mature lieutenant in "The Premonition," he is Ghost One Six in "Bringing in the Hueys," and he is the "buddy lieutenant" in "Albany."

And I speak about him. In my talks to groups about Vietnam and war, I never fail to mention Don Cornett. This is what I say: "When you, the members of my audience, go to The Wall, you see 58,000 plus names. I do not. I see Don Cornett's name 58,000 plus times. Because each one of those names perhaps had a mother, a father, brothers and sisters, a wife, and children. To truly appreciate the horror of war, multiply each one of those 58,000 plus names by nine or ten, because that's how many lives were shattered by the untimely death of the person behind the engraved name."

I promised his widow, Sylvia, who remarried another good man named Don after my friend Don's death, and to his son, Kevin, who tragically died of a massive heart attack at the age of 46, and to his sisters, Carol and Peggy, that I would never let the world forget Don Cornett. I also made the same promise to him, at his grave, and to myself.

I was privileged to know him; I am truly sorry that most of you did not. I am convinced that this country would be a better place had Don Cornett lived. And to this very day, I still miss him.

In 1998, his son, Kevin, and his widow, Sylvia, were presented the Silver Star for bravery, awarded posthumously, in front of Panel 3 East of The Vietnam Wall in Washington, DC. Don's Silver Star citation reads:

"For heroism while serving with Company C, 2nd Battalion, 7th Cavalry, 1st Cavalry Division (Airmobile), on 17 November, 1965, at Landing Zone ALBANY in the Ia Drang Valley of South Vietnam. First Lieutenant Cornett distinguished himself by gallantry in action while engaged in military operations involving conflict with a hostile North Vietnamese Army force. During this period, First Lieutenant Cornett, Company Executive Officer serving as Acting Company Commander while his own company commander had gone forward to meet with the battalion commander, walked overland with this company through the jungle en route to Landing Zone ALBANY in a battalion column of companies. The column came under an ambush attack by an aggressive, almost overwhelming, enemy force that attempted to split the battalion column and overrun the American force. His company took on the enemy's main attack. First Lieutenant Cornett attempted to free his men from the center of the killing field, stood up in a hail of enemy weapons fire and called out to his troopers 'follow me.' He was immediately shot twice, yet he continued to rally his company, and successfully got many out of the impact zone. He was hit and wounded a third time, this time mortally. His heroic act, in the face of an attacking enemy force was, however, directly responsible for saving the lives of several of his C Company troopers. First Lieutenant Cornett's gallantry in action, which ultimately led to giving his own life for his countrymen, and dedicated performance of duty were in keeping with the highest traditions of military service and reflect great credit on himself, the 7th Cavalry Regiment, the United States Army, and especially on the 1st Cavalry Division (Airmobile) which as a result of the victories achieved in the Ia Drang Battles won the Vietnam War's sole and the United States Army's fifth ever division level Presidential Unit Citation."

Don is buried in Section 35, Grave 195, Arlington National Cemetery in Washington, D. C.

Jim Lawrence

The author (right) and Lieutenant Don Cornett on board the USNS Maurice Rose passing through the Panama Canal on the way to Vietnam.

The Band Of Brothers

THE OLDER SOLDIERS BEGAN TO gather near the statue of the Three Fighting Men, the cold pre-dawn darkness hanging like a shroud over them. The glow of a smoke, a quiet mumble, a tug of the heart for what was about to happen.

The leader, with the quiet yet stern voice of command, gave the order to move to The Wall. The group, still bonded after all these years, passed silently down the walk. The Wall, beginning insignificantly on the left then growing in size and power as the band of soldiers moved toward the vertex.

Upon reaching their objective, the older soldiers began to huddle silently. No words were necessary to speak the bond and emotions of that moment. They moved toward each other, a hand on a shoulder, an arm to an arm, in a semicircle of brotherhood on that timeless spot.

The cold dark panel loomed over them, glaring

down the names of brothers who joined them in spirit at that great moment.

Heads bowed and eyes watered as the leader began reading the names. The catch of a breath in front, the quiet sob towards the rear, the exhale of the harbored hurt, as the memories flooded in, brought back by the names of men not recently spoken, but never forgotten.

The older soldiers shivered, partly because of the cold stillness of the early morning air, partly because of the call of the grave that emanated from the black granite panel.

The reading of the roll ended, some began moving away seeking a refuge from the cold of the morning and the burden of the heavy memory. But one of the older soldiers remained, staring at the panel, paying one last tribute as he went down the names.

This name the memory of a brave soldier who took a round to save a brother; this name the memory of a wife and baby left behind; this name the memory of a pilot who chanced the odds for one last pass. This name the memory of the bright young officer with so much promise; this name the memory of the beer-drinking buddy; this name the memory of the friend who fell on the live grenade.

The older soldier began to tremble, the power of the panel overcoming him. His cry, muffled at first, began to break the still of The Wall. He felt the same loneliness and loss that he had felt in the valley of the shadow of death so many years before.

At that moment, a hand on his left shoulder, another at his right arm. The fellowship, so evident years earlier, came again to guide and support.

The three older soldiers began to move away, one man guided by two brothers, just as the sun, providing the first beam of light, flickered over the dome of the capitol and past the tall bleak obelisk pointed towards the sky.

The three older soldiers walked away in the first warmth of the new day; a few more emotions purged, a little less guilt for having survived, the scars of their psyche soothed a bit more, with hopes to come again another day to share their burdens as a band of brothers.

The Band of Brothers, with family members, gather at panel 3E for the "reading of the names" ceremony at dawn on Veterans Day

Panel 3 East of The Wall, where the names of the troopers who were killed on both LZ X-Ray (1/7) and Albany (2/7) are located

AIRBORNE

"If I die on the old drop zone,
Box me up and send me home,
Pin my wings upon my chest,
Tell my girl I done my best."

The only place hotter than Airborne School at Fort Benning, Georgia in July... is Hell!

So here we were, the first day of week three of jump school. Week one—ground week, focused on physical training—getting into great shape, running in cadence, push-ups, sit-ups, and pull-ups. Covered with sweat, sawdust, and dirt, learning to land under a parachute—eyes off the ground and straight ahead, knees bent and toes pointed down. Learning to guide the chute by pulling and releasing the risers, going out of the 34-foot tower. Week one accomplished.

Then week two—tower week, more physical training. Miles and miles of jogging, doing the parachutist's shuffle, shirtless, in green army fatigue trousers and heavy black combat boots. The 250-

foot erector sets, the tall, metal towers, lifted up and released, hitting the ground under an open chute to apply what we had learned in the first week. Week two accomplished.

So here we are, sitting in the hanger down at the airstrip; ninety-eight degrees and humid outside, over one hundred degrees inside the old wooden building. Rows and rows of men seated on long, wooden benches. All dressed alike in their fatigue greens, all loaded down with combat equipment. A main parachute on the back, a reserve chute over the stomach, a heavy steel helmet on the head with a black student number stenciled over masking tape on the front of the steel pot. Four large and noisy ventilation fans way up high near the ceiling were taking hot air out and bringing more hot air in.

The bravado demonstrated by the students over the past two weeks was now replaced by a solemn quiet—eyes fixed, faces stiff as the nagging fear that kept most of them awake the previous night was becoming stronger as the hot July morning moved towards the moment.

I was seated in my numbered place, focused on two soldiers across from me. One younger, the face of a boy, still, quiet, determined. And his older buddy, bragging about what they were about to accomplish, talking about courage, bravery, heroism, laughing at the fears of his quiet, younger friend—but the insecure darting of his eyes told me who was the more afraid of the two men.

Suddenly, the command came to move to the aircraft. Sweating completely through my uniform and standing on shaky legs, I followed my stick, my numbered group of fellow jump students, out onto the runway. We saw the big airplane, the C-119, looking like a railroad boxcar with wings, a dual tail connected across the back, with two small doors on each side near the rear of the fuselage.

We boarded quietly, no one saying much now, but mental wheels spinning and guts wound tight with apprehension. The jumpmaster, barking commands, seated us in the proper numerical order, some seated down the middle of the aircraft, me and my stick with our backs against the outside of the airplane.

The two propeller engines choked, sputtered, and started, smoke washing down each side of the fuselage. The plane eased forward and taxied towards the end of the runway. The aircraft turned, stopped, revved its engines, then jerked forward. The plane gained speed, raced and rattled, sounding like every nut and bolt holding it together was coming loose.

I looked across the aisle and into the faces of my fellow students. The eyes told it all. Most of us were afraid. Some were already getting sick, the combination of motion and emotion already taking its toll. And I was absolutely sure that I looked just like them. Because this, my first jump, was also my first-ever ride in an airplane.

We lifted off and rattled skyward. I had this thought: "Why am I doing this? Why am I going to jump out of this perfectly good airplane when I don't really need to? After all, I am going to Vietnam with the First Air Cavalry, where all movement will be done by helicopter. I don't need this. Do you think the jumpmaster, a crusty old sergeant and master parachutist, will understand? Do you think he has been trained in apprehension counseling?"

Reason returned, and I logically deduced that the answer would be "No," so I sat quietly back in my seat. A soldier three or four to my right had just thrown up and the braggart, the one who had been cajoling his young friend back in the hanger, was in the process of pissing in his trousers, the warm yellow liquid running down into his boots, his face now pale with fear.

However, my attitude had changed abruptly. I was already tired of the shaking and rattling of the aircraft; I was offended by the smell of sweat, vomit and urine; so I wanted out. Let's get this over with.

The C-119 had leveled off and the jumpmaster

had moved to the rear beside the two jump doors. He was on his belly on the floor of the aircraft, looking outside, I assumed, for the drop zone.

Obviously seeing what he wanted to see, he stood up, faced us, saw the red light in the rear of the fuselage come on, and initiated the jump commands, both verbally and with hand and arm signals for those who could not hear over the noise of the airplane.

"Get ready!" he shouted, the order jerking us into the reality of the moment. "Stand up!" I wobbled to my feet, turned and faced the rear of the plane, my mouth dry like cotton. "Hook up!" I grabbed the metal hook of my static line in my right hand, reached for the anchor line cable with my left, and snapped the hook in place.

"Check static lines!" I looked at the static line of the jumper in front of me, making sure that it was not tangled or caught under his other equipment; I knew the jumper to my rear was doing the same for me. "Check equipment!" I checked the gear on my chest, including my reserve chute, then examined the equipment of the soldier to my front.

"Sound off for equipment check!" One at a time we yelled out our numerical position in the stick, meaning that we were now ready.

My mind was racing wildly; "So here I am. Can I

do this? Do I want to do this? This is crazy!" But the voice of reason and training overcame the fear; "Come on, soldier, you have been trained by some of the best teachers in the United States Army to do this, so do it! Suck it up and jump!"

At that moment the red light turned to green, and the jumpmaster gave the next-to-last jump command to the first two students in the stick; "Stand in the door!"

The wind was roaring outside the airplane. We were about 1,250 feet in the air and going very, very fast. The jumpmaster yelled "Go!"—that one short little word, the last of the jump commands. He tapped the first two students on the butt, and they were gone.

Each man in the stick then shuffled towards the two rear doors to fill the empty spaces left by the two jumpers, and the next two men stood in the door. I could only see the back of the soldier in front of me and I dared not look around him to see how far I had to go before my turn came.

We shuffled, we stopped; we shuffled, we stopped; the still quiet shattered by movement and commotion. Then suddenly, the man to my front took a left, stood in the door, was commanded to go, and was gone.

Now came my turn. The jumpmaster looked me

in the eye, a glint of satisfaction, a hint of power, but the caring of a teacher; pointed and shouted, "Stand in the door!"

I shoved my static line hook down the anchor line cable towards the very rear of the plane, took an immediate left, slapped each side of the open door outside the airplane with my palm and fingers against the metal, placed the toes of my jump boots over the edge of the door opening, looked out and thought, "Oh... my... God!"

Way, way down there was the earth, with its colors of brown and green, its neat patterns of well-kept fields and pastures broken up by the irregular lines of woods and streams. It was one of the most magnificent sights I had ever seen, but the jumpmaster did not give me very long to admire its beauty. I heard him yell the word, "Go!" knew it was meant for me, felt the slap on my butt, stepped out of the aircraft and into space.

The feeling I had might best be described as similar to dropping a very lightweight tissue in front of a large floor fan. The tissue falls slightly and then—zoom—it takes off in the fan's current. That is exactly what I did. I jumped out in my tight position, head down so that the jump bag would not hit the back of my head as it ripped away from my chute; my hands on my reserve chute, right hand on its handle, my legs straight and heels together.

The prop blast from the big propellers of the lumbering C-119 caught me and sent me flying, just like the tissue before the fan. Through opened eyes I saw flashes of green—brown—blue, earth and sky, with no sense or feel of up and down, as I counted, "Thousand—one," "Thousand—two," "Thousand—three," knowing that should I get to 'Thousand—four" without main chute deployment, that I had a problem and would need to rip the handle on the reserve, deploy it with my hands, or else become a little greasy spot on good Old Mother Earth.

Just as I got to "thousand—three," I heard and felt a pop, and all the spinning instantly stopped. I looked up and saw the full deployment of the beautiful olive drab main chute hovering over me like a giant, protecting hand. I was amazed how quiet it was up there. The aircraft was moving away so fast that it could hardly be heard. I also realized that almost all sounds are on the surface of the earth and that there is virtual silence one thousand feet up. Even the wind was quiet, since that was what I was riding.

Every now and then the silence was broken by the exhilarating yell of a jumper above or below me, but the peacefulness was incomprehensible. Just past my boot toes I could see those same fields, pastures, woods, and streams, but closer now. I also saw a large clearing with yellow smoke indicating the wind's direction on the earth's surface, the drop zone.

I began to maneuver my position by pulling and releasing the risers to the big chute, changing its shape and moving me over to the place I wanted to go.

The ground was coming up fast, so I began to ready myself for the landing. I assumed the proper parachute landing-fall position; waited only a moment or two, then a collision with the ground. I instinctively executed my parachute landing-fall and ended my jump all in one piece. Up quickly on my feet, I ran down the still partially deployed chute so that it did not drag me. My heart pounded fast in a rhythm of absolute joy for having done what I had just done.

Then I saw him. Jump Instructor Sergeant Sanchez—a Puerto Rican with narrow hips and waist, and shoulders, neck and arms about as large and as solid as I have ever seen. He picked me out the first day of the first week, saw my big yellow First Cav patch on my left shoulder with its black horse's head and bold, black stripe.

He realized that he, too, had orders to join the Cav in Vietnam; realized that he was a sergeant and I was a lieutenant; realized that someday I might be giving him orders, so decided that I was his for three weeks. He decided to give me pure hell while he had the opportunity.

The first day he saw me he had me drop to the push-up position and then barked, "Give me 1,000 push-ups, Lieutenant!" I did twenty or so until I fell on my face from exhaustion in the sawdust pit, but with the confidence that I had satisfied his sadistic cravings.

Much to my dismay, he took a piece of paper out of his uniform pocket, subtracted 20 from 1,000, and proudly announced that I owed him 980 more push-ups. For the last two weeks, every time he saw me, he would drop me for push-ups, take out that damn piece of paper, do his subtraction and walk away with a grin of great satisfaction.

Well, here he came. "Not now, Sergeant," I thought. "Not now. I know I've got a couple of hundred push-ups to go, but I've just accomplished some-thing really special, So don't ruin it for me, Ser-geant. Please, not now."

But the look on his face told me that he had something else on his mind; the look of mirth was gone, replaced by a much more serious mood. He walked directly up to me, stuck out his hand and said, "Congratulations, Lieutenant. I am proud of you."

He caught me off guard so I didn't know what to say. I simply nodded, thanked him, and continued gathering my equipment. He began helping me and as we walked off the drop zone together he spoke to me again, this time in the most serious tone I had ever heard from him, with an almost father-like quality in his voice.

"Do you know why you did this, Lieutenant? Why you learned to jump out of an airplane when you are going to war with helicopters?"

I shook my head and responded, "No, Sergeant, I really don't, but I have questioned that."

"Well, let me tell you why, Lieutenant. I made two combat jumps in Korea, so I know about this. The whole point of all this is not how to jump out of a C-119, but how to deal with fear and how to function while afraid. Combat is very different and you will experience fear like you have never felt before. Yet you will be in charge of men and your ability to lead them while afraid will determine whether they live or die. This ability will also determine whether or not you accomplish your mission. You are being trained to be under control and to lead while your emotions will be stronger than you can even comprehend. That's what this is about, Lieutenant."

I stopped walking, turned and looked at this man, placed my hand on his powerful, rock-solid shoulder, and understood for the first time what this sergeant from Puerto Rico really meant to me.

"Thank you, Sergeant; thank you very much. It has been a privilege to have you as my instructor. May God bless you. May God bless us all."

"If I die on the old drop zone,
Box me up and send me home,
Pin my wings upon my chest,
Tell my girl I done my best."

A. P. O. San Francisco

(Note: "A.P.O." is the postal abbreviation for "Army Post Office;" "A.P.O. San Francisco" was the mailing address for the United States troops in Vietnam and for free postage from the troops back to home.)

JUST OFF THE GREAT MALL of our nation's capitol, through the large doors of the museum of our history, to the right and up the stairs, down a long, dimly lit hallway, and in a glass case, you will find them.

His letters to her, on white military stationary, with the word "free" written where the stamp should be, scribbled in the abrupt handwriting of a young man laboring on a rough surface in a jungle base camp somewhere—opened—and read by her.

He was probably telling her about the heat in that oppressive hell-hole, the constant rain, the insects, the snakes, the bad food, the bad beer. Thoughts of home; his mom and dad, his little sister, his '65 burgundy Ford Mustang with the black vinyl top sitting in his daddy's garage; his victories on the ball field, his days in high school.

And her—especially her. About their night together after the prom; of watching the distant lightning of the gathering storm, hearing its rolling thunder, and seeing the sun rise. Her head against his shoulder, she pulled up tight against him in an all-night embrace. The aroma of her hair intoxicating him; of her smile, her touch, her eyes.

And of their plans when he got back home. A renewed courtship, a wedding, a family, a long, full life together in love.

His last letter closed with the exact number of days left in Vietnam and when he would be with her again. And the fact that his unit was leaving base camp for a jungle operation the next day.

Her letters to him, on feminine stationary, with delicate, faded flowers of pastels pink, blue, and green, still spotted with the long-ago stain of her perfume in the dainty hand of a young woman—unopened.

Perhaps containing words of trivial memories, promises made, future plans, and love offered; written as only she could write them, filled with emotions and feelings to encourage him to be careful and hurry home. But whose contents are known only to her and God.

Still sealed.

Never seen by him.

And now frozen in time, encased in this sterile museum environment, cold and unfeeling, perused by hundreds of intruding, foreign eyes; on display under glass for all the world to see but for no one to know.

With one other letter, on Department of the Army stationary; mailed to "Occupant," and insensitively and incorrectly addressed to her as "Dear Sir."

The letter read:

> *"The enclosed mail, addressed to Private First Class Stephen L. Bentley, bears your return address. I regret to inform you that he died on 17 November 1965.*
>
> *"Please accept my deepest sympathy over the loss of Private Bentley. I am truly sorry that it was not possible to have delivered this mail to him."*
>
> *Sincerely,*
> *Thomas C. Abbott,*
> *Lieutenant Colonel,*
> *Adjutant General Corps,*
> *Commanding*

Just off the great mall of our nation's capitol, through the large doors of the museum of our history, to the right and up the stairs, down a long, dimly lit hallway, and in a glass case, you will find them. These letters, left at The Wall by her, to remember and honor her young soldier whom she lost and will never see again.

Lieutenant Don Cornett with letters from home

Conversations With A Tombstone

THE OLDER SOLDIER STEPPED OFF the train, moved slowly upward by the escalator and out into a brilliant, crisp November day. He walked down the long, straight sidewalk, across the road and through the magnificent marble gates marking the entrance to the cemetery. He went past the sign asking for quiet respect to honor those buried there on the hallowed grounds.

The older soldier stopped momentarily, overcome by the contrasting colors of this place—the yellow, red, and brown trees, full in their autumn hues, reaching up to a bright, blue sky. The grass, still green, interrupted by rows and rows of small, white rounded tombstones, reaching out in all directions, neatly laid side by side and running parallel into eternity.

The older soldier began his climb up the steep roads void of any traffic, dedicated to foot visitors only. He walked past the tourists gathered around the tomb of the young president who was apparently going to keep them out of that hellish place until he was untimely struck down by an assassin's bullet.

He walked toward the Tomb of the Unknown; familiar only to God, and always attended by the members of the Old Guard.

The older soldier continued his climb, breathing more heavily now, knees and back beginning to hurt. These were problems he did not have in 1965 when he was humping the hills and jungles of Vietnam as a young, eager, infallible twenty-four-year-old.

Past the Tomb of the Unknown, around the curved sidewalk to the left, almost to the American flagpole, then off the sidewalk and down the grassy incline, through the rows of small, white stones to the bottom of the hill.

There, in a place the older soldier had stood many times before, in the shadow of the large, oak tree, he found the marker of his colleague and friend.

After a moment to catch his breath and gather his feelings, the older soldier spoke: "How are you, my friend? Here I am again, just as I promised. Every year, during our celebration, I've come over here alone to see you."

"Your buddies are just up the way. Older now, like

me. They are in the hotel hospitality suite, smoking and drinking; some telling lies, some avoiding the truth, some fighting the battle again, some purging their ghosts."

"Your name comes up a lot. You were brave, my friend. You earned the respect of your men and your country. You died doing…"

But the older soldier could go no further. The powerful emotion of this spot and this moment swept over him as it has done every year before. The older soldier's knees began to buckle, not from the walk, but from the stirring of his soul. His eyes filling with the tears of the loss, blinding him to the realities of the world.

He spoke again, but with much more emotion and conviction: "We really miss you… No, I really miss you. Do you remember those times on the ship going over, after lights out and the men were asleep. You and I would go up on the top deck and discuss everything—life, love, war, dying.

"We were the same age, but you were so much wiser. I really listened to you, tried to take your advice. You talked to me about being a good husband, about being a good father. You talked to me about war. You talked to me about dying, but I never believed it would come to this. Why?

"Why did you have to be the good soldier and seek

your radio operator as soon as the firing started? Why did you stand up to organize the counter-assault? They saw you, and it got you killed.

"Why was I the bad soldier? I could not find my radioman and became another foot soldier and defender. Just another rifleman. Why did the good soldier die, and the bad soldier live? I don't understand. I don't understand.

"But I miss your friendship. I need to talk to you. By man's standards, I have done all right. But to hell with man's standards! I've fought that battle over and over again a thousand times in my mind. Why did we not put our companies on line and assault the enemy to our right flank? Why did we not overrun the bastards and save all our men and return home heroes?

"But we didn't, or couldn't. You died, I lived. Who has it better? Who has it better?"

The older soldier paused, began to gather himself for his final words and departure: "Your wife and son are fine. I saw them last year. Like I have told you before, she married another good man who has taken care of her and your boy. But they still miss you. After all these years, they still miss you.

"I need to go now. But if you do not mind, I would like to pray."

(Ending #1)

The older soldier bowed his head. The last tear washing down his overcoat and onto the grass before the stone. "God, I pray once again for my buddy. I pray that he did not hurt long, that he died quickly, and that You pulled him into Your loving, protecting arms for all eternity. Lord, continue to look over his widow and son. Let Your guardian angel protect them until they can be with him again."

"And lastly, Lord, help me. I hurt, I feel great guilt, I am lonely... in a world surrounded by people at home and at work, I am so lonely. Give me comfort and peace, Lord, until I see You and him again, face to face. Thank You, God. Amen."

The older soldier took a few steps forward, past the foot of the grave, leaned over and reached out touched the rounded top of the tombstone. He whispered softly, "Good-bye, buddy, until next year." And started slowly back down the grassy hill into the starkness of reality.

(Ending #2)

But before the older soldier could start the prayer, a chilling wind blew down the hillside, through the trees, rustling the leaves into a whisper, and over the rows of gravestones. Was it the cold of coming winter or the cold of death?

The older soldier was taken aback. His words to God faltering, feeling an emptiness, a loneliness that he had felt before: "Why, Lord," he blurted out, "Why did You let this happen? If You are in control of the universe, then this falls on You. How could You let men hurt so? How could You shatter so many families?"

"They say You forsook Your own Son on the cross. I feel like You have forsaken us for years. What kind of a god is that? Who are You? Where are You? I am so lost!"

The older soldier stepped back, surrounded by the utter loneliness of that desolate spot, the cold wind cutting through him like the enemy's attack so many years ago. The conversation with his friend replaced by empty words bouncing off a lifeless tombstone.

(Ending #3)

Then . . . she appeared. Actually, she had been with me the entire time. From the hotel, on the train, through the cemetery gates, up the hill, past the guarded tomb, and down to this sacred spot. She had walked with me, yet kept her distance, given me my space, then stood behind me, watched me, hurt with me, cared for me, all with a reverent understanding that only she could sense.

But in my selfish grieving, I hadn't even noticed

her, hadn't even acknowledged her. Yet she was never offended by my ignoring her. Now, in my moment of frailty, weakness, and self-pity, she moved to me. I sensed her move even before she touched me; felt her coming up behind me. Her timing was perfect, just like everything else about her. Perfect.

She placed her left hand on my right shoulder, raised my right arm with her other hand, and slid under my raised arm, pulling it tightly around her shoulders, and laid her head on my chest.

She then joined me in the prayers, joined me in my grief, and joined me with her tears. She was silent, still, solemn, but her presence was overpowering; me looking down at the tombstone, she looking up into my face.

Then, she waited. Waited until I was through, waited until I was finished with my visit. Again, reading me perfectly, and without a word, she took my hand, grasped tightly in hers, and led me away. Down the grassy incline, under the tall trees, then to the left up the steep paved road. Sensing that I was still weak, still shaken, she guided me to a wooden bench just down the hill from the Tomb of the Unknown.

Again took my hand in hers, slowly rubbed the back of my trembling palm, moved close to me, so close that her breath mingled with mine, and softly whispered, "It's OK. I'm here. I'm with you. I've got you. It's going to be all right."

We sat there on the bench a long time, silent, looking across the great river at the capitol city of our nation. Two people isolated, surrounded by millions, one comforting the other, soothing the wounds, mending the scars, bandaging the fractured soul.

She understood. She understood me completely. She knew me better than anyone else. And she taught me, and I learned. I learned that grief shared is so much less painful than grieving alone.

She's gone now. Maybe to another man. Maybe to another soldier. Maybe to another war.

Was she real? Was she imagined?

I think she was real. I know she was real.

And she's out there. I know she's out there.

Don Cornett's grave stone at Arlington National Cemetery

The author visiting the grave of his friend, Lieutenant Don Cornett,
at Arlington National Cemetery

The grounds of Arlington National Cemetery near the grave of Lt.
Don Cornett

A Voice From
The Wall

I RAN MY FINGERS ACROSS the name of my brother fallen years ago, feeling the edges of the engraving of that cold black rock. I shuddered at the loss. The tears began to well. I shook my head at my inability to proceed. The fear of the loneliness returned like a thousand times before. The burden of surviving filled me with pity as I trembled there.

Suddenly a Voice from The Wall spoke to me with a clear strong sound. Startled at the intrusion, I attempted to pull away, but my hand held to the name on the panel by the force behind The Wall.

I recognized the Voice of my fallen comrade:

"Soldier, what is wrong with you! Why do you stand here and wallow in your self-pity! You were no different from me. We were both soldiers, you and I. We were both good men but the bullet found me and not you. That is the only difference. I was meant to die, you to live. There was a purpose in my dying, and a purpose in your living. Yet you burden yourself with having survived. You have carried your grief and guilt for all these years. Those around you suffer because you have focused only on yourself and your loss. Come on, soldier, get over it!"

The Voice was scolding and stern, speaking words that I hated to hear because I knew it was speaking the truth. The words cut deep into my being, past my protective cover of silence, past my survivor's guilt, past my horror of the experience, past my paralyzing fear never forgotten, and into my soul and heart.

The Voice sensed the defeat of my barriers and the falling of my soul. It came again, but this time with the understanding, the consoling tone of a friend.

"Also know that my pain, though intense, was quick. Yet you have suffered for a long time. You have hurt for me and considered yourself lucky for having survived that horrible battle. I am not sure that I agree. Maybe I was the lucky one. My plight was short, but your agony continues."

"So do us both honor by finding your purpose. Learn from my death. Spend some time in remembrance of those of us who died that November. As the leaves fall from the trees and the cold winds warn of winter, spend a quiet moment thinking of us."

"But that memory must not consume you. Move from the past to the present, then glimpse into the future. Honor me by moving others ahead of my memory. Pay heed instead to those of the present. Be a thoughtful husband, a loving father, a good neighbor. And, most of all, a vibrant patriot—one on fire with the spirit of our country. Stand tall when you hear the Anthem, feel the emotions when you salute the flag, support your survivor brothers and our families we left behind."

"One more thing, soldier, one very important thing, and then I will let you go. Remember this— we did not lose, we left. The politicians lost. We paid the price, you and me. We were good soldiers. We went over there and fought our battles because our leaders called. We gave for our country because we believed in its purpose. This is all that we could do."

"So raise your head, soldier, and walk away proud. Take our honor and courage, proven on the battlefield long ago, into a world that desperately needs it now. There are more battles to fight, so do us proud, soldier, do us proud."

THE MAN AND THE DEER

I WATCHED A MAN SHOOT a deer once. The man fired, the deer fell; its head jerked two or three times as if to grasp a few, last precious breaths. A small stream of blood oozed from its mouth, and then came that straight-ahead, unblinking stare, looking mindlessly into the nothingness of death.

The deer was born, the deer ate, slept, grew, reproduced, and died.

I shot a man once. I fired, the man fell; his head jerked two or three times as if to grasp a few, last precious breaths. A small stream of blood oozed from his mouth and then came that straight-ahead, unblinking stare, looking mindlessly into the nothingness of death.

The man was born, the man ate, slept, grew, reproduced, learned, thought, philosophized, became angry, became evil, hated, worshipped self, hurt others, killed, and died.

I killed a man once.

I don't think I could kill a deer.

THE MOTHER

THE BOY'S MOTHER PULLED INTO the driveway after another hard day at school. The junior high kids were as unruly as ever, but today she did not notice. They noticed, though; they saw her there in body but realized that her thoughts were thousands of miles away.

Out of her car, across the lawn, her steps mechanical, thoughtless. Up the front porch of the house, past the afternoon newspaper which she would normally pick up and carry in for her husband. But not today, not this day.

* * *

The eighteen-year-old private, his body shattered by the exploding mortar round, lay in the tall grass. His life blood oozing out of the cuts and gashes caused by the metal fragments. "Mama," he called. "Mama."

* * *

She moved down the hall, past the dining room

and kitchen and into the den. She went straight to the television set and turned on the evening news.

The same news broadcast of the previous day reported the battle—a furious ambush of an American battalion by the Peoples' Army of Vietnam. She had just received a letter from her son; she knew he was there, knew it was his unit that had been attacked.

She sat on the sofa, oblivious to her surroundings, oblivious to her husband's presence, he clutching another double bourbon and water to help him overcome the news that they were both about to watch.

* * *

The twenty-four-year-old lieutenant lay with his face in the dirt, his helmet shattered, his head pressed against the hot earth. An automatic weapon had fixed him in its sight and hit him four times. The intrusions tore through his vital organs, and he waited on the ground to die. "Mama," he moaned. "Mama."

* * *

The television commercial ended, the news program began. The reporter, clad in jungle fatigues, began his breathless report: "Straight from the battlefield, with the first pictures of the slaughter.

An American battalion was ambushed two days ago...."

She saw the very scenes she dreaded—the carnage, the shattered weapons, the shattered bodies. The survivors solemnly carried their loads, wrapped in the olive-green body bags, to the waiting helicopters.

The reporter was now quoting the numbers, the emotions of his voice heightened by the power and impact of all that was around him.

* * *

The thirty-nine-year-old sergeant, machine-gunned six hours earlier, lay on his back, looking up through the jungle canopy at the last light of the fading day. His pain having subsided, dulled into the moment of death as his life passed away. "Mama," his plaintive call. "Mama."

* * *

Then she remembered. Horrified, she jumped up from the sofa, went straight to the television screen, and spoke to the news reporter as if he could hear her. "Please, please," she begged, "He was so afraid of the dark when he was a little boy. Terribly afraid!"

She was crying now. "Please don't let them zip

it up. Please don't let them zip that bag all the way up! Please don't cover his face with darkness. Please, not the blackness of the bag! Oh, let the light shine on his eyes, his beautiful eyes, his beautiful eyes...."

Then the call came.

THE STARE

The author sitting on the "horse" of the First Cavalry Division, Airmobile, the UH-1 Huey

THE RADIO CRACKLED, THIS TIME with orders to get the company ready to lift off and replace our sister battalion which had been on the ground fighting for their lives for two and one-half days on that hot landing zone.

I had been able to monitor the progress of the

battle on the same radio that was ordering us in right now. It had been two and one-half days of hell for our brothers. Choppers and planes shot down, many men wounded and killed. The enemy had penetrated the landing zone more than once. The fighting was hand-to-hand at times, but the Americans had held fast. By God, they had held fast.

The hueys were approaching us, making that familiar chopping, egg-beater sound. We moved from our pick-up position as our helicopters touched skids to ground, the dirt and grass swirling about us, stirred by the chopper blades.

We loaded in, the fear we had already recognized now being heightened as we jumped on our ride into war. I put on the headphones as the leader of the group, tapped the pilot on the shoulder indicating that we were loaded, and he lifted off.

Over the static of the phones and the noise of the blades the pilot spoke, tired but focused: "All right, lieutenant, you are going into a red hot landing zone. The enemy has the clearing surrounded so we will be going in at tree-top level. You can expect enemy fire as we approach the LZ. Men have been hit on almost every approach."

Suddenly the pilot laughed, a tone of bravado to hide the persistent fear. "But don't worry, lieutenant, you won't be able to hear the incoming rounds over the noise of the chopper. You won't know you're hit until they hit you. High pucker factor, lieutenant, high pucker factor. So just suck that nylon seat right up your ass and enjoy the ride!"

We lifted up high and fast. I could tell by the confident way the pilot handled the ship that he had done this many times in the last two and one-half days. I saw immediately the gray and white smoke of the embattled landing zone, contrasted with the dark green of the surrounding highland jungle and framed by the large, abrupt mountain.

We came in hard and tight, clipping the tops of trees with the chopper's skids to avoid the enemy's ground fire. The helicopter touched down in the middle of the dusty, smoky clearing. The men and I off-loaded, making room for some of the soldiers of our sister battalion who would be coming out of this hellish place.

I hit the ground in a crouched position, my automatic weapon at ready, expecting to have to fight our way to the other friendly forces.

Then I saw him, walking slowly towards the chopper, completely oblivious to anything happening around him, an expression on his face devoid of any feeling. And his eyes—his eyes—the eyes of a nineteen-year-old, going on sixty. A stare that struck more terror in my heart than the fear of an enemy bullet.

What had he seen? What had caused this cold, lifeless stare in these once young blue eyes? Perhaps he had seen his buddy, head split and shattered by an enemy machine gun round. Perhaps he had seen his platoon leader holding his own guts in his hand after being raked by automatic weapons fire. Perhaps he had heard the nightly cries of the wounded men in front of his fox hole, the low moans of men slowly dying on the quieted battlefield.

Perhaps he had expended himself, exhausted from the intense emotions of combat, with little food, little water, and no sleep. Perhaps he had sighted down the barrel of his weapon, fixed the enemy soldier in his sight, squeezed the trigger, and seen the man's head explode.

Perhaps he had.

Perhaps he had.

He had.

I have often wondered what happened to that boy. I wonder if he went back to the States, to his home, his family and friends. And I wonder if they noticed the change, that his laughter was hollow, that he smiled very little, that his dreams were vivid and disturbing, that he could not love as easily as before.

I wonder if he married, had a family, ever brought his wife and kids to The Wall. Told them about some of the names inscribed there, about how they lived and how they died. And I wonder, as his kids stepped forward with pencils and paper to take markings of some of the special names described by their father, I wonder if the stare returns.

THE PREMONITION

THINGS WERE QUIET NOW ABOARD the ship. The men were asleep down in the bowels of the big gray troop transport. The two young lieutenants, as they had done almost every night, headed for the top deck. They walked past the cramped mid-deck area where they had conducted physical training with their men earlier in the day, past the officers' mess where they ate their three daily meals and attended classes in the Vietnamese language, small unit tactics, battlefield first aid, and a myriad of combat-related topics.

Up the narrow metal, backless stairs, clutching the handrail as the ship pitched and rolled in the great Pacific Ocean as it approached the South China Sea. They moved across the wooden deck floor over to the two rickety deck lounge chairs they had occupied so many evenings before. Under the deep, black shadow of the giant, gun-metal gray smokestack, painted with the large yellow and black patch of the First Cavalry Division, the horse's head looking forward in anticipation of what was to come.

The wooden chairs clattered as the two young lieutenants positioned themselves to look up past the faint string of lights and the flying cinders from the smokestack. They looked up into the dark sky, now illuminated with millions of bright stars. The constellation Orion, the Hunter, had his shield pointed towards the west, the direction that the ship was heading—not to protect himself from Taurus the Bull but from the war that was only a few hundred miles away.

Even though the two lieutenants were born just one week apart, they were years different in age.

The first one was mature and accomplished; an outstanding athlete in college, married to a beautiful woman and the father of a darling baby girl. He was a man with it all together and a mentor to the second.

The other young officer was immature, socially and physically, and relied heavily on the first for advice about life, love, death…. No, not death—it was a topic they now avoided.

They both sat back in the deck chairs, lit cigarettes, and pulled the first few drags long and hard. The red glow lit their faces, knowing that this privilege would vanish in the jungles of Vietnam. They knew that all an enemy sniper would need were a couple of face lights from the drag of a cigarette to put a bullet between their eyes.

The second lieutenant spoke first: "You know, after this is over, and I get home, I'm going to look for a woman as much like your Sharon as I can find. You are a lucky man, lieutenant, a lucky man. She is a looker, she is a great cook, and she is a great mom to your little girl." Then, with a note of sarcasm and humor in his voice, "You don't deserve her, lieutenant. She's too good for you."

The first lieutenant smiled at his buddy, knowing that he was right, but knowing that she was so much more than his friend even knew.

"And she is a great lover," the first lieutenant responded, "And I mean so much more than the act of lovemaking. She loves me, and she shows it every day in everything she does. We truly love each other, and she had a very difficult time of it when we loaded the buses at Fort Benning bound for Charleston. I've been thinking about that, all the way through the Panama Canal, past the refueling at Long Beach, past the Hawaiian Islands and heading towards Southeast Asia. I've been thinking that this war may be as difficult on them as it might be on us.

"And I don't want her to hurt, I don't want her to fear, and I hate leaving her alone. We two have truly become one flesh, one spirit, one soul, and it seems so unnatural now for us to be apart for a year or more."

The "or more" struck the second lieutenant strangely, but he said nothing.

The first lieutenant continued: "But Sharon and I did not become complete until little Amy was born. Oh, that little girl, that little girl."

The first lieutenant put his head back against the wooden deck chair, closed his eyes, smiled in reflection, and spoke softly: "You cannot imagine the feeling when that little girl stumbles over to me, crawls into my lap, looks up into my face, and calls me 'Daddy.' That's the first word she learned to say, and still the sweetest sound out of her mouth."

He ceased speaking, and the second lieutenant envied the satisfaction of fatherhood that had become so important to his buddy. At the same time he was thankful that he, as a single man, did not feel the awful burden of separation that obsessed his friend.

But then, another thought, a different thought, clouded the second lieutenant's mind—one that was nagging every young officer on the ship: "Do you think you'll be afraid? Do you think you'll be able to lead? What will you do when somebody is shooting at you and trying to kill you?"

The first lieutenant snapped out of his moment of bliss into the reality of the present: "If you mean combat, sure, we will experience fear. Sure, we'll be afraid, but we've been trained to function, trained to lead in combat, so we'll be all right. And we'll support each other.

"Our men are well trained, they will be proud fighters and they will protect us, just like we care for them. We are both just twenty-four, lieutenant, but we two have earned the respect of our men. So we should be... we should be...."

The first lieutenant stopped in mid-sentence, now staring past his buddy and out towards the blackness of the ocean depths and beyond. He began to shake and moan, then began a quiet crying, a reaction the second lieutenant had never seen from his more stable buddy.

"I'm not going to make it, I'm not going to make it; I'm never going to see my wife and daughter again!"

The second lieutenant looked on incredulously as his friend continued: "I've had this premonition for weeks. I couldn't tell you, I couldn't tell anyone, but I just know it. So I'm going to ask a great favor of you. Please see that my wife and child are taken care of, please see that they...."

The second lieutenant interrupted, angry at his colleague's reaction and scared at his statement. "Stop it, now stop that! You don't know. You don't know what's going to happen. You don't know a thing about combat. Many men have fought in many wars and many have survived to go home to their wives and children. So get that thought out of your head right now!"

The second lieutenant stopped, surprised at his own boldness in chastising his friend and now really afraid about what was going to happen to both of them.

They sat silently for a long time, the only sounds that of the great ship, moaning and groaning as it rolled, cutting through the black ocean. The sounds of the salt spray hissing as the hull sliced through the waves of the dark sea.

The first lieutenant slowly rose to his feet, extinguished the light of the last cigarette, and quietly announced, "I'm going to sleep."

The second lieutenant got up, patted his buddy on the back, and both went down the steps into the darkness of the depths of the dull gray ship to rest.

Lieutenant Don Cornett in deck chair on top deck of the USNS Maurice Rose in happier times on the way to Vietnam

Bringing In
The Hueys

"LONE RANGER SIX, THIS IS Mule Train Six. Over."

"Hey, Lieutenant, did you hear that? Mule Train Six is calling!" said Private Ansley, my radio operator.

My recon platoon had just air assaulted somewhere east of our base camp in the central highlands of Vietnam and somewhere southwest of Bong Son. We had only been in country a month and a half, carving a home out of the jungle near An Khe, and getting ready for war. This was our first operation in the field and maybe our first combat experience.

Recon had hit the ground first; my 34 troopers and I had secured a very large, flat landing zone about the size of two football fields. It was almost perfectly rectangular in shape with no trees, bushes, or any other growth except tall grass. It was surrounded by thick, dark green hedgerows, five to eight feet high, patterned as if planted by man as opposed to being a free-growing forest.

I had noticed a Vietnamese village as we approached the LZ by helicopter. The village was now to our southwest, about one-half a mile. Directly north of our location and down a six to eight foot drop was a fast-moving stream, about ten feet across and no more than a couple of feet deep.

On the other side of the stream loomed a very tall stand of palm trees, stretching from east to west almost as far as the eye could see. They were darker at the top due to the intermingling of the tree-top canopy; an ominous, wild-looking place.

An unknown that sent a cold shiver down my spine.

My recon platoon had secured the landing zone. One squad was southwest towards the village, one squad north towards the stand of dark palms, and one squad to the east.

My platoon sergeant, radio operator and I had moved into the hedgerow to the north.

"Lone Ranger Six, This is Mule Train Six. Over."

"Lieutenant, it's Mule Train Six, it's The Man, Lieutenant!"

Each unit had its own radio call sign. Recon was

"Lone Ranger." The number "6" meant the leader of the unit. I was "Lone Ranger Six." The call was coming from "Mule Train," not my Delta Company commander, a captain who, in the chain of command, would normally be calling me, but from "Mule Train Six," the battalion commander, the colonel himself, The Man himself.

"Lone Ranger Six, this is Mule Train Six. Over." And this time, "Over" was said with irritation in his voice.

I grabbed the handset of the field radio, pressed the talk key, and responded, "Mule Train Six, this is Lone Ranger Six. Over."

"This is Mule Train Six; I have a mission for you. Galloping Ghost is inbound to your position, about 15 minutes away, and we had to relocate the Pathfinders to another LZ about a half mile to your east. A little problem over there, so you are going to have to bring Galloping Ghost in. Do you understand? Over."

My heart jumped into my throat. Galloping Ghost—Charlie Company, 2nd Battalion, 7th Cavalry, 1st Cavalry Division, Airmobile. And the colonel wants me to bring them into my LZ to begin our first combat mission in Vietnam. Yes, I had been trained in air assault techniques at Fort Benning, and yes, I am the recon platoon leader. But this is for real. I felt very insecure, very small, at that moment in time.

"Lone Ranger Six, this is Mule Train Six. Do you copy? Over."

"Ah—Mule Train Six, this is Lone Ranger Six. Ah—I copy that, I'll bring them in. Over."

"This is Mule Train Six. Out."

The order was given and it was final, now the job was mine. The battalion commander had just handed me one of his three rifle companies, Galloping Ghost—Charlie Company. And the colonel expected me to accomplish my mission, to bring them in. So be it.

My platoon sergeant, Sergeant Bentley, had monitored the radio conversation and was ready. Bentley was a small, thin man, but rock-solid inside and out. The men loved him and respected him. He was the perfect platoon sergeant for a young, wet-behind-the-ears, just out of ROTC, second lieutenant like myself.

"Let's go, lieutenant! We've got a job to do!"

The sergeant grabbed the radio from the operator, strapped it on his back, locked and loaded his M16, and stepped out from our hiding place in the hedgerow onto the clear, flat surface of the landing zone.

As the two of us moved out onto the LZ, I took the handset from Bentley and attempted to raise Galloping Ghost.

"Galloping Ghost Six, this is Lone Ranger Six. Over."

The company commander of Charlie Company, a captain, responded, "Ranger Six, this is Ghost Six. I have been monitoring your transmissions with Train Six so I know what's going on. We are about ten minutes out. I am going to hand you over to Ghost One Six. He is in the lead chopper. He and his men are the initial assault. Don't screw this up, Ranger Six."

"Galloping Ghost One Six," the platoon leader of Charlie Company's first platoon, was a second lieutenant like myself and my best friend in the army. We had been roommates in Infantry Officer Basic Training, roommates in Airborne School, and roommates on the ship coming over to Vietnam.

What do you know! The first air assault in the Vietnam war by the 2nd Battalion, 7th Cavalry was being directed by two 24-year-old second lieutenants.

"Lone Ranger Six, this is Galloping Ghost One Six. Over." I instantly recognized my buddy's voice and I smiled for the first time.

"Ghost One Six, this is Lone Ranger Six. How are you? Over."

"This is Ghost One Six, inbound from the south. The chopper pilot wants you to mark your position with smoke. He needs your location and wind direction. Over."

I responded, "Roger that. Be alert for the smoke. Out."

My platoon sergeant and I moved a short distance to the northerly part of the landing zone. A bright, hot sun shined down out of the Asian sky. My uniform was already soaked through with the sweat of the hot, humid Vietnamese morning and the tensions of the moment.

I carried only my M16 strapped over my shoulder so that my arms were free to direct the chopper pilot. Sergeant Bentley was right behind me, no further away than the length of the handset cable of the radio on his back.

I looked south, into the southern sky, and way, way off, I saw the sky filling with dozens of small, black dots, the Huey helicopters carrying Charlie Company—inbound to my location.

Then something amazing happened.

A large clod of red-brown dirt jumped out of the

ground and bounced off the back of my right leg. My jungle fatigue pants were sprayed with grains of sand.

"What was that, sergeant? Did you see that!"

"We are being shot at, lieutenant! There is a sniper out there! He must be behind us! He just missed us! I've got your back!"

Sniper.

A lone man with a high-powered rifle, probably with a scope attached. The ultimate combat experience in the fear of the unknown. You don't know where he is, who he is sighting down on, and when he will pull his trigger next. You can't see him and you can't hear him until his next shot. If you are lucky enough to be looking in his direction when he fires his next round and you see his muzzle flash or the smoke from his rifle, you can find him. And if you are lucky enough, you won't be hit by his next bullet. Because, if you are, it won't matter.

"Lone Ranger Six, this is Galloping Ghost One Six. The pilot requests that you pop your smoke. Over."

"Ghost One Six, this is Lone Ranger Six. We've got a sniper down here. Victor Charlie is somewhere out there so I guess we have a hot LZ. Over."

A long pause, radio silence, then, "This is Ghost One Six. Roger hot LZ. Throw your smoke. Over."

I took the olive drab canister off my web belt, grabbed the pin with my left hand, pulled the pin, and threw the smoke grenade off to my left. I felt a slight breeze coming from the west and I did not want the smoke interfering with my line of sight.

The grenade began hissing as soon as the handle popped. As it hit the ground, bright orange smoke began billowing up from the LZ. The black dots in the southern sky were larger now. Looking like black tadpoles, round, fat bodies with long, thin tails, and I could barely hear the faint yet familiar "Whomp-whomp-whomp" of the inbound Hueys.

The loud, splintering crack of the air just over my head, a sound similar to dry wood snapping, told me that the sniper had us in his sights and had just missed us a second time. I wanted to run back to the safety of the hedgerows, find this guy, and take him out. But I could not leave the LZ with Charlie Company inbound.

My gut was tied in knots with the stark fear that the sniper was lining us up for a third shot, and there was absolutely nothing I could do about it.

"Lone Ranger Six, this is Ghost One Six. We see green smoke and orange smoke. What gives? Over."

"This is Ranger Six. Negative on the green smoke! Negative on the green smoke! Come to the orange smoke! But hurry up! We've got a hot LZ here! Over."

"This is Ghost One Six. Coming to the orange smoke. Understand a hot LZ. Coming as fast as we can. Out."

I thought, *Green smoke, green smoke—who's throwing green smoke. Is it our Pathfinders over on the other landing zone bringing in someone else, or is it the bad guys trying to confuse our chopper pilots?*

"Lone Ranger Six, this is Galloping Ghost One Six. The pilot has informed me that we have an escort of gunships. He is sending in a couple of armed Hueys that are covering us to help you with the VC and to make our arrival safer. Can you give me some direction? Over."

"This is Lone Ranger Six. Looks like one sniper, probably to our north. North of the orange smoke, across a stream, probably concealed in a forest of tall palm trees. He has us zeroed in so we could use your help. But tell the gunships to be extra careful, I've got men in the hedgerow just south of that stream. Over."

"This is Ghost One Six. Pilot tells me to tell you that they are on their way. Keep your heads down. Out."

And here they came. Two armed Hueys, loaded with rockets and armed with machine guns, coming straight at me from the south. And looking like flying demons from hell.

The lead ship fired his rockets long before he reached the landing zone. Watching them launch from the armed platforms on his sides, the rockets zoomed and swished over our heads, trailing white smoke, and exploding in the palm tree line just across the stream to our north. He then raked the tropical forest with machine gun fire before he banked hard to the left.

The second ship duplicated the aerial assault of the first. We watched the palm thicket literally disintegrate before our eyes. The ground below was showered with broken palm leaves, palm bark, other greenery, and hopefully the body of the sniper.

I turned back to see the slicks, the Hueys, loaded with Charlie Company just a few hundred yards short of the landing zone, so I prepared to bring them in.

I handed Sergeant Bentley my M16, took a deep breath, faced the lead ship, and thrust both my arms straight up into the air, the palms of my hands facing each other, meaning, "Come to me." I heard the radio crackle and Sergeant Bentley said, "They have you."

Here he came, the lead Huey in a stick of four. The other three ships were guiding on the lead chopper that I was directing.

The pilot brought the lead chopper over the hedgerows to the south, his skids almost touching the tops of the hedges. He slowed his ship down, nose slightly up, tail down, coming right at me, not more than 15 feet above the ground. What was once a little black silent dot in the distant sky was now a loud, very intimidating military machine, dark green in color, with a large yellow 1st Cavalry patch painted on its black nose.

Speed still slower, distance still closer, guiding on me with my arms stretched upward, now seeing the pilot's face under the helmet and goggles. The powerful machine, now stirring leaves, grass and dirt, some beginning to blow into my face, as the troop-carrying helicopter came straight at me— now only a few yards away and only a few feet above the ground.

I dropped both my arms straight out from my body and parallel to the ground, palms down, indicating to the pilot that he was over his spot. The pilot slowed the aircraft, hovering over the touch-down position but still a few feet up in the air. I now had him where I wanted him. I could see that the other three ships were over the large, rectangular landing zone, so I dropped my arms to my side, telling him that it was clear to put down.

And he did.

The split second that the chopper's skids touched dirt, the men of Charlie Company began to off load. The troopers in the lead chopper being led by my good buddy, Ghost One Six, who was the first one off.

He immediately began dispersing the men of his rifle platoon into the hedgerows to the west. He glanced at me, smiled, gave me an enthusiastic "thumbs up," and then ran off with his Charlie Company troopers.

I looked back at the lead chopper pilot. I knew that it was not wise for them to stay on a hot LZ for long, so I saluted, then gave him the infantry "move out" arm signal. He saluted back, revved his machine, took the Huey several feet above the ground, then slammed the controls forward. The black nose of the chopper, the bright yellow Cav patch with the black stripe and the horse's head, came right at me.

I ducked—partially out of habit and partially out of necessity. The powerful ship roared just over me, its skids almost within arm's reach. Then he banked sharply to the left and was gone.

The other ships followed and were quickly gone also.

Except for the noise of the men of Charlie Company moving through the hedgerows and out into the fields beyond, their leaders barking orders in the distance, the landing zone was strangely quiet.

I looked back at Sergeant Bentley, a great sigh of relief as I exhaled slowly for the first time in a long time. He said, "Let's go, L.T. That sniper may still be out there."

The renewed reality of the threat caused both of us to sprint back into the protection of the hedgerow and our little command post.

I laid back into a cool, dark depression in the ground, hidden from any eyes by the dense hedge, and reflected on the previous 30 minutes. A feeling of complete exhilaration came over me as I realized what had just happened. "Wow," I thought. "Wow!"

"We did it. We brought them in. The cavalry came. On their 'horses.' But this time, the 'horses' were Hueys, fast, accurate, mean machines, helicopters carrying men into battle. The 1ˢᵗ Cavalry Division. The First Team. Airmobile. Wow!"

The radio crackled, "Lone Ranger Six, this is Mule Train Six. Over."

"Mule Train Six, this is Lone Ranger Six. Over."

"This is Mule Train Six. Good job, son. Out."

Recon Platoon Sergeant Ron Benton, Delta Company, 2/7—who was the prototype for "Sgt. Bentley" in "Bringing in the Hueys" - and Recon Platoon Leader Jim Lawrence, Delta Company, 2/7 CAV

Did You Know, Mama?

DID YOU KNOW, MAMA? JUST tell me, did you know?

Did you know when I was swimming around safely in the warm waters of your womb, when I was drinking the life-giving milk from your breasts, when you tucked me away at night, hearing my bedtime prayers, "Now I lay me down to sleep, I pray the Lord my soul to keep; If I should die before I wake, I pray the Lord my soul to take." Did you know there were others who would try to take my soul?

When I was a child and skinned my knee, you would treat the wound and dry my tears. When I feared the dark and the monsters you would calm my fears. When my Daddy came from work, from the perfect job to the perfect home to a perfect life in a prefect time, did you know?

When I went to grade school, in perfect fellowship with my buddies, with no cares, no obligations, just fun times; when you sent me to military college where they prepared me for leadership, for discipline, for patriotism, for devotion, for duty, honor, and country—did you know?

When I went into the army and trained in military organization, tactics and strategy, but no training in fear, killing and death, when the aggressors in field exercises were firing blanks as we played war games just like I did as a kid playing cowboys and Indians—did you know?

Did you know when you sent me over there that I would come face-to-face with hundreds of men who would try their very best to kill me? That they would fire weapons emitting a spinning, metal projectile that would destroy my muscles, my flesh, my organs, my bones. That they would fire rockets and shells that would dismember me, tear my arms and legs and head from my body. That they would run up to me as I lay wounded in the tall grass, see that there was some life left in me, and, as I looked up to them with pleading eyes, put a pistol to my head and plunge me into eternal darkness. That they would take that bush hook, that harvesting tool, and desecrate my body, the very same body that you took such skill and care to raise. Did you know, Mama?

If you didn't know, Mama, if you were naïve like me, if you didn't really think that people could act like that and do things like that to other people, especially towards your boy, because you thought your boy was special, then it's OK.

On the other hand, if you did know, if you learned lessons from your great war and if you knew that the leaders of our country were making decisions over cups of coffee while perusing their newspapers in their white house, decisions that would destroy individuals and families, then why didn't you just tell me?

If you knew that life was just a dirty trick, that you raised me into thinking that all was safe and good and perfect, but there were those out there who would brutalize and devastate me, that my innocence of youth would be shattered by the experience of the world and the evil of mankind, then you should have told me.

Unless...

Unless...

Unless...

You knew of something else, someplace else, someone else.

The Gold Star Kid

THE OLDER SOLDIER STOOD IN front of his panel, the third panel to the right of the vertex. The black granite stone looming large and powerful over him, he stood as he had many times before, his hat pulled low across his forehead to protect him from the chills of Washington in November and the influence of the moment before him.

He stood with his arms crossed over his chest, a defensive posture, protected by the long overcoat—close enough to read the names, but far enough to avoid the full power of The Wall.

His group of names, in chronological order as of date of death, clustered together from that other November day in 1965.

He looked at a name. Then, in his mind's eye, a face, a shape, a hometown, a family, a story, and how he died. Then to the next name, repeating the process until all sixty-four names had been silently honored by the older soldier.

He was oblivious to all the activity around him,

another Veterans Day, with the members of the press corps carrying their pads, tape recorders, and cameras. The school children on their field trip, laughing and giggling off the bus but somewhat somber now in the presence of The Wall, and not knowing why. The citizens of Washington and beyond, there to honor those who paid the ultimate price. The active soldiers wondering if they will ever get the chance to fight their war, excited at the opportunity but already afraid that it might come.

And the veterans, some dressed inconspicuously, like him, and some still wearing the uniforms and medals of the engagement—displaying an outward, visible symbol of all that has been bottled up within them. Their intricately embroidered denim jackets, the brightly colored threads showing maps, places, dates, and slogans of a horror past. Tattoos, chains, boots, beards and ponytails speckled with gray, hiding a face but never hiding the anguish seen in their eyes.

The older soldier continued to stare and reminisce when a young man stepped between the soldier and his panel. He looked to be in his early thirties, broad shoulders, rough hands, a three-day beard under closely cropped hair.

Annoyed at first by the intrusion, the older soldier took one step to his right to continue the grieving process when he noticed the young man shudder and heard the broken exhale of one near grief. He had seen this reaction before and knew that the young man was at The Wall for the first time, and had finally found the name of someone significant.

The older soldier continued watching. Shifting his focus from the list of the dead to the crisis of the young man, he saw him take a step towards the panel, slowly raise his right arm and lovingly drag his fingers across a name.

The name was one of the sergeants in the older soldier's unit, a man who was killed just a few feet away from the older soldier's wounding. As the young man dropped his head, fingers still in affectionate contact with the engraved name, the older soldier moved forward and placed his hand on the heaving shoulder of the stricken youth.

The young man turned abruptly, the moment of grief broken, but in anticipation of the contact, with a look of incredulity showing through the tears in his eyes.

The older soldier spoke: "I am sorry to intrude, but I could not help but notice that you touched Sergeant Comer's name. May I ask why?"

The young man took a deep breath to gather himself; blinked away the last tear and spoke: "Yes, sir—Sergeant Comer was my Dad, but I really didn't get to know him because I was only two years old when he died. My Mother would not speak of him and would not let my brothers and sisters speak of him. The others were all right with that, but I have never been satisfied so I had to come here.

"I had no money for this trip but a veterans' organization in Alabama raised the money and paid my way. I rode a bus to Washington. I was told to go to the tent, the tent for the Gold Star Kids, to get some information, but no one seemed to know what to do.

"Then an older woman with a gentle voice and a kind face told me to go to my father's panel at The Wall, that someone would be there who served with him and would know about him."

The young man hesitated, then asked, "Did you know my Dad?"

The older soldier was now moved by the moment. He knew what was about to happen. He took a deep breath himself, looked into the eyes of the young man, and responded: "Yes, I knew your Dad. I was with him when he died."

The young man took a step backwards, shuddered again, let out a quiet sound as if seeing a ghost: "Are you serious! Are you serious! The lady was right! She said you would be here! Please tell me about him; please tell me all you know about him!"

The young man stared expectantly as the older soldier gathered his thoughts: "Your father was a sergeant and I was a lieutenant, so we did not spend much personal time together, but I can tell you a few things. He was a good soldier, a good leader, a good man, and...."

A smile crept over the older soldier's face, "He was one hell of a softball pitcher. He and I sat on the bench after winning the post championship at Fort Benning, drinking a beer in celebration. Your Dad was the star; he was the best player on the team."

The young man smiled for the first time, then asked his next question: "What did he look like? My mother had thrown away all of his pictures... what did he look like?"

The older soldier gathered his courage for the impact of his next response and spoke: "Go look in a mirror and you will see him. The structure of your face, your smile, your eyes, are just like his. You are his boy."

The young man teared up again as he saw, for the first time, his father's face in his.

After a moment of composing himself, the young man summoned the strength for one last question, the question that had eaten at him all of his adult life: "Sir, did he die a man?"

The older soldier had anticipated the question and was prepared to answer. The moment of truth upon them both: "He died fighting the enemy who had surprised us on Landing Zone Albany with a horrific ambush. Your Dad was one of the ones who helped turn the momentum of the battle. He died facing the on-rushing enemy, standing and firing his M16, and, I'm sure, taking out many of them before he went down. He not only died a man; your Dad died a hero."

For the first time in over thirty years, the young man breathed a sigh of relief, purging his own ghost that had haunted him since his youth.

A look and feeling of contentment swept over him, a feeling that he had never felt before, finally fully satisfied with the older soldier's story.

But the older soldier was not through: "There are many men who served with your father and were in the battle when he died staying at a hotel near here. We get together every year at this time. Would you like to meet them and learn more about your Dad?"

The young man, now overwhelmed with the possibility of meeting many soldiers who knew and fought with his father, simply nodded.

And the older soldier and the Gold Star kid, now two men with one purpose, walked away from the panel and up the sidewalk to a long-anticipated reunion.

The gathering at The Wall on Veterans Day

Cav color guard (closeup) standing above Panel 3E of Wall

Just Don't Ask Me

JUST DON'T ASK ME. DON'T ask me about the war. I cannot—I will not—tell you. You see, there are reasons I can't talk about the war.

First, there are no words that can adequately tell you, words do not exist that can describe what I saw, what I felt, what I did.

You have not experienced combat, so there is no way I can express my feelings, my experiences. The more I would say, the less you would understand.

I cannot express the hurt, the hurt of death, and how quickly it can devastate. You may have experienced death, the death of grandparents, parents, spouse, child, or friends; but most of those deaths were anticipated. But for us soldiers, even though we were in combat, and expected to be shot at every day, you never thought it would happen to you or to your men. It was always something you would hear about, but an event and concept so foreign, you just didn't comprehend. So when it came to you and your men, and came so fast, and came so ruthless with such a horrible face, you cannot express it. It's no use to try.

And fear. There is no way to tell you the fear one feels in the most intense moment in combat, when you realize that you are probably going to die, and that your own death is going to be a painful and gruesome death. There is no way to describe the fear that encourages, even begs, you to run, to leave all behind just to save yourself, yet why you cannot answer that call, because you have been trained not to run but to function, to lead, to act, to prevail. You are ashamed and afraid, both at the same time, and that fear is so powerful that it reaches down inside of you and grips you so tightly, grabs your heart, your soul, your gut, your bowels, that you feel you are going to puke and spray your soul all over the ground.

Everything good inside you, your thoughts, your ideals, your manners, your customs, everything learned, everything patterned, all carved away, leaving only a skeleton of a self, and the horrible creature of fear that now so dominates your being. I will not tell you; you cannot understand that.

And the memory. The memory that never passes away, as hard as you try every day, every damn day, to dispose of it. The memory of aiming your weapon, steadying your hand, sighting down on the man, squeezing the trigger, firing the rifle, and watching the man's body devastated by the projectile fired from your rifle. And the eternal knowledge that you just killed a man; ended the life that he and others had spent years building. He can no longer see, he can no longer think, he can no longer laugh, he can no longer cry, he can no longer love. He can only rot away, all because of you. And the lives of his parents, who loved and raised him, are forever changed. And the life of his wife, who also loved him and misses him, is forever changed. And the lives of his children, who need him and revere him, are forever changed. All are denied any more time with him, never again to see him alive, all because of what you did.

And finally, because of what I saw, because of what I did, I now have inside of me a creature of the most horrible proportions, a monster that resides in the dark, dark recesses of the attic or the basement of my soul or mind; it is shackled and sleeping. At times, the bonds are tight and the sleep is deep; it is constrained by the shackles of customs and courtesies, of rules and laws, of right and wrong. But at other times, the bonds are only loosely locked and the sleep is not a deep sleep; its breath is shallow and its eyes roll. I do not want to awaken it, to stir the miscreation from its slumber, because I know what it can do. I have seen its power and fury, and I am not going to provoke it again.

So don't ask me about the war. Just don't ask me.

It's All Over

THE LIEUTENANT AND THE CAPTAIN had been gone from their base camp in the central highlands, their wartime home for the last nine months, for three days. Three days spent in the small room of the officers' quarters at the big airbase just outside Saigon. Venturing out of the room only to eat and relieve themselves, avoiding at all costs the nearby temptations of the thriving Asian city and the dangers that also lurked there.

The stories of American soldiers shot by the Viet Cong riding bicycles, and hand grenades being rolled down the aisles of movie theaters, and the hurts inflicted by the women of the night who were sympathetic to the other cause.

No, these two men were short-timers, having survived some of the fiercest battles fought in the central highlands. They had demonstrated courage and bravery uncommon to man, but an everyday trait of the cavalry trooper. They were now nervous and shy as their time in country was reduced from weeks to days to hours.

Then they were on an early morning ride to the air strip, wearing khakis for the first time in a long time instead of the olive drab or camouflaged jungle fatigues that they had worn for almost one year. Then aboard the shiny silver airplane, the first hint of home, instead of the brownish, green troop transports of the war.

The two soldiers settled in their seats, glanced up and beheld, for the first time since the Bob Hope Show came through their base camp... an American woman.

The flight attendant, normal looking by most standards but beautiful to men who had grown accustomed to the high-pitched, nasal voices and the beetle-nut dirtied teeth of the diminutive native highland women, walked down the aisle of the plane. She spoke gently to the two soldiers who were still staring at her face and body but saying nothing, and asked them to buckle their seat belts.

As she passed on by, the captain muttered to the lieutenant, "Buckle the seat belt! Hell, lieutenant, we've been flying into hot landing zones on bullet-riddled Huey helicopters with the outside doors removed, jumping out before the runners touched the ground, receiving incoming rifle and machine-gun fire, while firing back and killing the enemy. And she wants us to buckle our seat belts!"

"She's just doing her job, captain, so let's make it easy on her and enjoy the ride."

The lieutenant buckled his belt and settled back into his seat while the captain, still grumbling under his breath, complied with the request of the beautiful flight attendant.

Just then the pilot's voice over the aircraft's intercom broke the silence with a surprising message: "Gentlemen, welcome aboard flight 767, scheduled for immediate departure from Tan Son Nhut airbase to Oakland, California." A rustling and a muffled cheer went up on board at the mention of the Stateside location. "We have just been radioed that some aircraft taking off right before us have received some small-arms fire at the end of the runway, so you will notice a steep banking to the left as soon as we lift off in order to avoid taking any hits. Welcome aboard."

The two men looked at each other, an expression of disbelief on both faces. "After all we've been through, lieutenant, I'll be damned if I'm going down in this steel box!" And the captain unbuckled his seat belt, ready to jump out at a moment's notice.

The pilot taxied the big silver bird down to the other end of the runway, turned, revved his engines, and slammed the stick full forward. The plane lurched and rumbled down the pot-holed runway. The men felt the wheels separate from the ground, then a quick, steep turn to the left. The two soldiers once again felt a twinge of the fear felt so often in combat, still yet another moment of truth defining life or death in the tensions of the instant.

The airplane gained elevation and began leveling off. The captain, seated by the window, looked outside and watched the lights of the runway, the air base, and the city fade in the distance as the two soldiers and all their on-board buddies were being spirited away from the war.

The pilot's voice again came on above the roar of the engines, but this time with the sweetest message imaginable: "Gentlemen, we received no ground fire and therefore took no hits. We are leveling off over the South China Sea. Gentlemen, you have just left Vietnam. Your war is over."

A loud roar engulfed the entire cabin area as hundreds of men simultaneously experienced the lifting of the heavy burden of the Vietnam conflict that had been oppressing them every moment of every day since they had been in country. The captain quietly reached over, shook the lieutenant's hand, and said with a tear in his eye, "Congratulations, son, you have made it. God bless you, you have made it. We left so many like you there; too many like you went home in body bags and boxes. But you, son, made it out of there. Now, take some advice from a captain, don't go back. Once is enough. You go home and find a purpose in your life. Go back to a country that loves you. You have been blessed with life when so many others have died. This is going to be a long war where many more like you are going to fall. Don't be one of them. Don't go back." The captain then closed his tired eyes, lowered his head on the head rest and went to sleep.

The flight home was uneventful. The plane landed in Oakland, the captain and the lieutenant parted company, and the lieutenant went through debriefing and out-processing at the Oakland Army Terminal. Upon leaving the army facility, the new civilian hailed a cab with the idea of going across the bay and spending a few days in San Francisco. The former lieutenant, excited about his departure from the military and wanting to talk about his newly gained freedom to anyone who would listen, told the cab driver to just take him to a nice hotel that might have a vacancy, then began telling the cabbie about his experiences as an officer in the United State Army in combat in Southeast Asia. The cab driver, a dark-skinned man who spoke broken English, seemed to know very little about the war in Vietnam. In fact, the ex-lieutenant was taken aback by the fact that the driver didn't even know that there was a war going on. So the young man, disappointed, sat back in solitude for the remainder of his ride across the bay.

The cabbie dropped the ex-lieutenant off in front of a fairly nice hotel in downtown San Francisco. He paid the cabbie the fare, received no response, picked up his one small bag, and went inside the hotel. He approached the check-in counter, asked a somewhat homely young woman if they had a vacancy, got an affirmative response, and initiated the process to rent a room. Again, excited about his new freedom and his past service to his country, he began telling the young girl about his wartime experiences in Vietnam. She looked up disinterested, heard him out with a somewhat bored expression on her face, and then replied, "That's nice. I've put you in room 214." She handed him a key and then turned and walked away.

Dropping off his one bag in the hotel room, he decided to treat himself to a really nice meal in the hotel's restaurant. After being seated at a table with a slightly stained white linen tablecloth and sterling silverware, the ex-lieutenant was approached by a waiter, a tall, thin man with a long, expressionless face and dressed in a black and white outfit resembling a tuxedo, with a black clip-on bow tie that was tilted to the left. Again, being excited about his new life as a civilian and wanting desperately to talk to another civilian about it, the young ex-officer addressed the stoic waiter. "Man, you do not know how excited I am to be sitting here in your fine restaurant and getting ready to eat some real food! You see, I've just left the army, having been in combat in Vietnam for almost a year, and I can't wait to start this new phase of my life!"

The waiter, a bored look on his face, spoke with almost no feeling; "You mean, that police action over there. Which side were we on anyway—the north or the south?" Without waiting for the ex-lieutenant to respond, the waited said, "What would you like to order?"

And for the first time, the young ex-officer realized that the people back home, with the exception of family and close friends, had no idea what was going on in Southeast Asia, and could care even less. He had been in a battle where over 150 of his colleagues had been killed and over 120 wounded, including himself, but nobody knew and nobody gave a damn. Now, in his first day as an American civilian, he felt alone, isolated, unacknowledged, and unappreciated in a city of millions, whose freedoms he thought he had fought to protect. And, for the very first time, he asked himself a question that he has asked himself a thousand times since then. Why?

DEAR JOHN

EVEN BEFORE THE AMBUSH STARTED, his only thoughts were of her; she had preoccupied his every wakened moment, but now more than ever.

Yet here he was, a young officer in charge of a rifle platoon made up of enlisted men and non-commissioned officers looking to him for orders and direction to get them out of this killing field of devastating fire of the enemy ambush.

As he lay face down in the sharp, tough elephant grass, only a few hundred yards or so from the promised helicopter pick-up point, the clearing of the landing zone, he was torn between his duty as a lieutenant, the platoon leader, and his loss as a husband.

As the bullets cracked only a few feet over his head, and the deep thump of exploding mortar rounds, the clash and clamor of nearby hand-to-hand combat, the shrieks and screams of battle, his focus was blurred.

"How could she? How could she? Does she not

know I'm doing this for her? Does she not know I'm defending her freedoms and privileges as well as all the rest?"

He closed his eyes, his face down in the hot, sandy grass, and saw her. Of average height but athletic build, smooth olive skin, sandy blonde hair, a natural contrast with the sun-darkened complexion, and green, green eyes, camouflage green, concealing behind them the quiet, mystical nature that he had found so attractive when they had first met, but never could quite penetrate and fully understand in their two years of marriage.

He could also see her delicate hand, moving slowly and carefully as she transferred her thoughts to paper, and writing the words that had brought tears to his eyes only days before:

"Dear John,

I do not know exactly how to tell you this, but I cannot go on this way; you left me here alone while you pursued your war. I have heard things and read things since you left me four months ago, things about your war, things unpleasant, things horrible; that you and your soldiers are killing men who are defending their homeland, and killing innocent civilians in the process; you are the invader, the aggressor, against a people who have been defending their country since the French invaded in the fifties.

And I have met a man who has told me all this, who has convinced me that you are fighting an unholy war. He is not like you; he is kind and sensitive, he does not like killing of any kind, but talks of peace and brotherhood and love.

And he loves me in a way you never could. So as much as it hurts me to write this letter to you, I must tell you that I am in love with him and plan to marry him as soon as we can finalize the divorce that I filed yesterday.

We had some good times together, and you will always be a friend, but I truly believe that this will be the best for the both of us."

She signed it "love," but he knew that any love that had been there was gone.

"How could she?" He thought again, "Doesn't she understand? No, she doesn't understand—doesn't understand that I am here in this hellhole by choice, sent by my president, my commander-in-chief, to defend our way of life, our democracies, our freedoms, against a cause that would limit all rights and freedoms. Doesn't she understand that I was sent on a mission by my father, as a savior . . . a savior . . . ."

The confusion created by the heightening battle sounds of the dead and dying and the empty images of her and the words of her letter now drove his thoughts to days long ago, to his youth, to serving the priest as an acolyte at the altar of God.

The images and words of the communion service flooded in, the bread—the wine—the flesh—the blood—"Eat, this is my body which was given for you, do this in remembrance of me.

"Take this cup—this is my blood which was shed for you…"

Then he understood, now he knew his purpose, his role; he knew what he must do to save her, to win her back, to keep her soul from everlasting damnation.

"I do this for you, my darling, I do this in remembrance of you; this is my body which I give for you; this is my blood which I shed for you: I do this so that you will remember me."

He laid his heated weapon down by his side, smoke still curling from the barrel; he removed his steel helmet and carefully placed it beside his rifle, and rose from the ground, away from the safe cover of the tall elephant grass, and into the interlocking crossfire of the enemy gunners.

He stood fully erect, stretched out both his arms with palms up, beckoning towards Heaven, with the imagined nail holes in his hands, and mouthed the words, "Forgive her, Father, for she knows not what she does." A look of serene peace on his face just as the enemy machine gunner recognized his new target of opportunity, aimed, and fired.

SHE'S OUT THERE

SHE'S OUT THERE.

I know she's out there.

I did not become aware of her until I reached manhood, when playmates became girls and girls became women. I was aware of her in high school, but she distanced herself far from me; then in military college, where the girls from the elite private boarding school and the nursing students of the state university showed me bits and pieces of her. But all fell short.

I really became aware of her when I went to war. On the transport ship going over she and I would spend time together under the magnificent array of stars blanketing the night sky, she and I alone on the darkened top deck. Then on ambush patrols in the dense jungles, shivering and soaked through by the seasonal monsoons, way after midnight in the hazy darkness of the pre-dawn, she would come to me, hide with me while we waited for the enemy to enter the trap.

Sometimes, as I lay on my back in the sleeping bag on the jungle floor, my pup-tent mate long since asleep, snoring the stillness away, I knew she was looking up into the same sky, seeing the same full moon, watching the same falling star, even though she was on the other side of the globe back home. Other times she would come directly to me, quietly slide into my sleeping bag, nestle her head and long hair against my shoulder, my arm around her back, her leg thrown across mine, and hold me so close, so still, so long.

In the hospital after my wounding, after lights out and the ward deserted, she would come sit beside my bed, take my hand, wipe my brow, silently watch me, assuring me that all would be well.

Even now, when I'm down, when the demons in my head are stirring and the battle starts all over again, she senses my hurt and comes to me, understands my loss and consoles me. Without saying a word, she takes my head in her arms, strokes my tired, unshaven face with tender caresses and caring hands.

She brings peace into a world of hate; she brings quiet into a world of confusion; she brings relief into a world of pain; she brings calm into a world of fear.

What does she look like? She has green eyes, eyes as blue as the clear summer sky, as brown as the deep woods; her hair is long and dark, blonde as the bright sun, red as the autumn leaves; she is fair skinned, dark skinned, white and tanned.

She is exotic, elusive; she is ethereal, eternal.

Where is she? She is here, and there; everywhere, nowhere; she comes, and she goes; she is of the moment, yet outside of time.

Who is she? She is comfort, she is concern, she is understanding, she is consoling, she is touching, she is holding.

She is love unconditional.

I have been waiting for her. I have been looking for her, for a long, long time.

She's out there.

I just know she's out there.

The Valley Of The Shadow Of Death

LIKE ALL ARMY OFFICERS, THIS captain was well trained. He had learned basic infantry small unit tactics, he had been prepped in battlefield strategy, especially in guerrilla warfare; he had been specifically trained in the employment of helicopters and the innovative techniques of the airmobile concept when his infantry unit at Fort Benning, Georgia, had been converted to the First Air Cavalry Division; he had learned some of the Vietnamese language on the ship coming over and was an expert rifleman.

As an army chaplain, his training had gone much further. He knew how to conduct religious services in the field; he was an experienced marriage and divorce counselor; and he had had some grief counseling training. He was, he thought, about as well trained as an army chaplain could be.

But he was not prepared, not prepared at all, for what awaited him inside the large tent that he was about to enter.

The very spacious hospital tent was capable of holding twenty-five to thirty tables upon which the stretchers of wounded and dying soldiers could be placed. The tent was only a few yards from the helicopter landing pad, so the tent side flaps were down, keeping out the dust, sand, and debris stirred up by the incoming choppers carrying their heavy loads and keeping in the darkness that concealed its horror.

Although the battle had been going on for four days, the dead and wounded of the Second Battalion, Seventh Cavalry, those ambushed on the second landing zone, were just now arriving. Some of the wounded, those with hand, arm, and shoulder wounds, walking off the helicopters; some with leg, hip, and foot wounds being carried by their fellow soldiers; the more seriously injured brought in on stretchers or wrapped in their own ponchos.

Then there were the dead. Their bodies also encased in their ponchos, but with the heavy rubberized dark green rain gear pulled up over their faces to hide the distorted expressions of the final moments of agony. A few already zipped up in the ominous body bags.

As the Chaplain opened the flap door to the big tent, his eyes took a few seconds to adjust to the musty darkness, but his sense of smell reacted immediately to the indescribable odor of suffering and death that awaited him. Off to his right as he entered were small teams of doctors working on the wounded, those who held some hope of surviving; their gruesome tasks illuminated by small lights on stands being powered by the outside generators whose hum was muffled by the large, heavy tent.

Over to the left were those more seriously wounded, those the doctors gave little or no chance of surviving that living hell; being attended by medics and aids to make them as comfortable as possible, with the faint hope that some miracle might save them but with the stark reality that their time grew shorter every minute.

Down at the far end of the tent were the dead; recovered disfigured and jumbled from the battlefield, but now laid in orderly rows, quiet and still, and being attended by no one.

The Chaplain blinked and quietly gasped as his eyes adjusted to the horrible sights before him and his mind adjusted to the profound psychological impact of the dreadful moment. He began to move from stretcher to stretcher, wanting to help the doctors but staying in the shadows out of the way so that the medical personnel could perform their gruesome tasks.

As he stayed back, watching the fantastic scene unfold before him, the doctors operating quickly and efficiently but in a heavy, dark atmosphere of silence, as if in reverence to the dead and dying, he heard a quiet voice behind him, over to the left side of the tent; he heard someone call his title.

"Chaplain…. Chaplain."

The Captain turned and saw, through the dim, dusty light, an arm raised, bent and bloody fingers up, from a stretcher near the tent wall, beckoning him to come.

As he approached the table, he recognized the grizzled old sergeant, a senior, non-commissioned officer, a Korean War veteran, with a wife and several grown kids back in the States. The sergeant had been wounded twice in Korea, had received several decorations for valor, and had the reputation as one of the toughest in the battalion. He was hard, but he was fair; he had prepared his soldiers for combat, had made boys into men, and his soldiers loved him.

He lay stretched out on his poncho that was draped over one of the six-foot by three-foot tables; he lay on his back, his head tilted slightly in the direction of the Chaplain; his jungle fatigue shirt ripped open and his olive drab tee shirt cut away to reveal several holes in his chest, the results of small arms automatic weapons fire.

A couple of rounds had torn through several vital organs while a third bullet had pierced his lungs, causing a sucking, bubbling sound every time he breathed.

The Captain walked over and carefully took the beckoning hand, looked down into the face of the dying man and said without much though, "How are you, Sarge?"

"Not so good, Sir. I've been hit pretty bad. But you know what, Chaplain, I'm not hurting like I was, I'm not hurting as bad. That's strange, isn't it? Really strange."

The Chaplain took a deep breath, still trying to comprehend the scene before him, and trying to get his nerves under control. "What can I do for you, Sarge?"

The sergeant quietly responded: "Chaplain, you know that I haven't been much of a religious man, that I haven't been to many of your church services, and I apologize for that; and I'm afraid I took the Lord's Name in vain way too many times, and I apologize for that too. But, Chaplain, I need something."

"I can remember when I was a little boy growing up in Alabama, that my Mama, God rest her soul, would get me up on Sunday morning, get me dressed, and take me to that little wooden white church out in the country. I remember that preacher, more than once, talk about a place, a place called The Valley of The Shadow of Death. Do you know about that place from The Bible, Chaplain? Can you tell me about that place?"

The Captain continued to gather his thoughts; "Why do you want to know about The Valley of The Shadow of Death, Sergeant?"

The Sergeant took his eyes away from the Chaplain, looked straight up into the darkened heights of the tent; a look of fear came over his face as he recalled the tragic events of the past twenty-four hours, shuttered from his head to his toes, and said with conviction; "Because I think I've just been there, Chaplain, I think I've just been there."

The Captain had recited the 23rd Psalms many times, but never under circumstances such as this. He took another deep breath as he struggled to overcome the emotions of the fretful moment with the pressing need to be under control and thoughtful. He saw the words in his mind's eye and began:

"The Lord is my shepherd;
I shall not want."

The wounded soldier shuddered again, the mixture of air and blood bubbled up out of his chest as he inhaled another precious breath and looked at the Chaplain's face as he recognized the familiar words.

"He maketh me to lie down in green pastures;
He leadeth me beside the still waters;
He restoreth my soul."

The Sergeant took a longer, deeper breath, still accompanied by the horrible sounds of the chest wound, nodded in agreement and quietly repeated: "He restoreth my soul, He restoreth my soul."

The Chaplain continued:

"He leadeth me in the paths of righteousness
For his name's sake.
Yea, though I walk through
The valley of the shadow of death…"

The wounded soldier became visibly excited, reached up in pain, grabbed the Captain's fatigue jacket, and said loudly, "Yeah, that's it, Chaplain! That's the place! I just left there, Chaplain! I've just been there!"

The Chaplain, shaken to his very core, could only continue with the memorized words:

"Yea, though I walk through
The valley of the shadow of death,
I will fear no evil:
For thou art with me;
Thy rod and thy staff
They comfort me."

The Sergeant had settled back down, gazing again at the top of the darkened tent, breathing slower and less deep, the bubbles of blood from the chest wound now much smaller than before. He quietly muttered the words: "I will fear no evil . . . . He restoreth my soul."

The Chaplain saw the peace stealing over the hurting soldier and moved towards the conclusion of the Psalm:

"Thou preparest a table before me
In the presence of mine enemies:

Thou anoinstest my head with oil;
My cup runneth over."

The Chaplain glanced down, saw that the soldier's eyes were fixed upward in a non-blinking stare, saw that the bloody bubbles had ceased coming out of the holes in his chest, and saw that a very slight smile had crept over his face as his mother took his hand and led him to that small church in the country, and finished his recitation:

"Surely goodness and mercy
Shall follow me all the days of my life:
And I will dwell in
The House of the Lord forever."

FIELDS OF FIRE

WHEN THE SOLDIER HEARD THE first scattered shots coming from across the landing zone where the recon platoon and two platoons from Alpha Company had gone into the wood line, he was confused; he thought that all the damage inflicted on the enemy on Landing Zone X-Ray should have sent them running, but somebody was firing at someone, and he was confused.

He was also tired and hungry and felt that he did not need any more delays from a cold shower, a hot meal, and a comfortable bunk, so he was annoyed by the scattered actions from across the open field to his left front.

Suddenly the well-concealed enemy opened fire from the soldier's right flank, springing the surprise ambush perfectly and pouring small arms fire, automatic weapons fire, rockets and mortar rounds into the startled American column.

The soldier dropped into the tall elephant grass, shocked at the turn of events, feeling fear for his life at the sudden assault, but experiencing the transition that must occur in a combat soldier at a time like this.

His old self—his feeling, caring self—his hungry, tired self, began fading away, and the other persona, the one that the United States Army had spent time and money to create, was kicking in.

His eyes glazed over, his brain began to click automatically, and now he began to understand fully why he spent three arduous weeks in Airborne School in repetitious training to be able to jump out of perfectly good airplanes when he was assigned to the First Cavalry—Airmobile, a unit that moved exclusively by helicopter; why he had gone to Ranger School and suffered through the hell of the mountains and swamps to earn that little arched yellow and black tab. Now he knew, and the fighting man was asserting himself; all the repetitions, all the training, so that the sensitive, caring man of thought would give way to the cold, calculating man of action.

He raised his helmet-covered head enough to determine that the enemy was to his right, that the Americans had been surprised and were being decimated by the enemy's blistering crossfire; that the enemy would try to close with the Americans quickly, and that he had to do something.

He looked and saw a nearby anthill, a clay-hardened mound of dirt about six feet tall and six feet round at the bottom and tapering to a pointed top, which would provide good cover for his body while allowing him to expose his right eye—his shooting eye, his right arm and shoulder, and his M16 automatic rifle. So he moved quickly in a crouch to his anthill—his combat station—and fell into the rhythm of his combat training, the mechanics of his body performing without question the need and duty to fight back.

He slid up against the anthill, above the tall elephant grass, so that he could establish his fields of fire and seek his targets of opportunity. At that very moment, the North Vietnamese soldiers came out of the wood line to the American's right flank with the sole purpose of closing with their enemy, neutralizing their air superiority and artillery, and annihilating the foreign invaders.

The American soldier saw the enemy, picked out his first target, locked and loaded his M16, chambered the first round, pulled the black plastic butt of the weapon deep into his right shoulder to absorb the recoil, grasped the black plastic stock with his left hand while rotating his left elbow under the weapon to steady it, clicked off the safety, set the selector switch to semi-automatic, sighted down through the two sights, aligning the triangular front sight blade in the center of the rear sight, began to squeeze the pistol-grip handle and the trigger, stopped his breathing halfway through the exhale, and fired three quick shots.

The enemy soldier dropped, shot squarely through the chest and dead before he hit the ground. The soldier sighted on another, followed the exact same procedure, and another enemy fell. Then another. Then another.

Suddenly the top of the anthill mound was splattered by several machine gun rounds, and the American to the soldier's right was hit in the neck and head and went down screaming. The soldier peered out around his mound, looked up into the dark green canopy of the tall jungle trees and saw the muzzle flashes of the enemy machine gun.

The training—shoulder, sight, exhale, hold, squeeze—pow, pow, pow. The enemy machine gunner fell out of the tree, down until his harness caught him and left his dead body dangling fifty feet up in the air, hit by two of the three rounds fired by the American fighting man.

The soldier looked back towards the wood line, still feeling nothing, but reacting as he was taught; he saw three enemy charge out together, with bayonets fixed on their Chinese-made AK-47 assault rifles; they were only fifty yards or so away, so the soldier knew it was time. The man on his right was dead, the Americans to his left were wounded, so this was his gunfight, his shootout.

So he entered the zone—the killing zone—not a place, but a state of mind; devoid of reason, devoid of logic, devoid of fear; composed of the mechanics of his training, his strong sense of survival, a pressing desire to win, and the arrogance of a fighting man who knew he was indestructible at that moment in time.

He clicked his selector switch to fully automatic, stepped out from behind his hiding place, standing completely exposed to the enemy, muttered "rock and roll" once under his breath, and sprayed twenty rounds of high-velocity death into the charging enemy.

All three went down, clattering and tumbling to the ground; but one got back up, three small red dots now in the middle of his khaki-colored jacket and his silver belt buckle with the red star shattered by a fourth bullet. He started towards the American, stunned and shaken, a look of amazement on his face, but going on guts. The American fighting man calmly ejected his empty magazine, locked his weapon, loaded a full clip, unlocked—sighted—squeezed—fired, the North Vietnamese fell again, only to get up a second time, to be put down again by the rifleman's third volley.

Then, almost as suddenly as the ambush had started, it stopped. The soldier just stood there as the mass confusion and noise of battle was replaced by an eerie quiet; except for the groans of the wounded and dying, a strange silence fell across the battlefield, a scattered shot or two off in the distance, but the battle was over.

As the smoke began drifting away, the man of action, the one trained for all this, began crawling back into the shadowy depths of his soul, and the other person began to re-emerge.

The soldier looked around him and saw the carnage of combat; he saw the shattered weapons and the broken bodies, the dead hanging from trees and the groups of bodies from both armies piled together in a hand-to-hand fight to the death, and there he stood without even a scratch.

And he knew that he was now two people, and he would always be two people; first the one that the public would accept, the one that would conform to society's standards, that would hold the right job, go to the right church, raise the right family, say the right things, live the life that all back home expected him to live.

But he also knew that he was another person, a soldier trained for combat, and one that would always lie just below the surface of the first persona, and never very far away. He knew that he would have to hide the second person, that the first person would have to control the second, partially because the world would not approve of the thoughts and actions of the second person, partially because the first person might not be able to bear the thought pictures of the horrible slaughter, partially because no one could ever understand what he had experienced; he knew he would never talk about the battle, he knew he would not even try to explain, he knew that only those who had been there could understand, and he knew that he would spend the rest of his life as two persons, and most would never ever know.

Two A1E Skyraiders came to the rescue of the 2/7 on LZ Albany. The bravery and accuracy of the two pilots averted an even greater loss of American lives on the ground.

LZ Albany

THE YOUNG LIEUTENANT KNEW THAT his men were tired. They had been monitoring the death fight of their sister battalion on that hellish landing zone named X-Ray by radio and rumor for two days.

Then they had choppered in to relieve the remnants of that brave unit; seeing the dead bodies of Americans and North Vietnamese, smelling the horrible stench of bloated corpses rotting in the hot highland sun, shattered weapons and shattered lives all around them; their feelings heightened, then dulled, by the aura of the aftermath of that great battle.

Now they were walking away from that landing zone, exhausted from lack of sleep and little food and water, but elated to be leaving that bloody, godless place.

The young lieutenant knew vaguely their orders. The captain had explained that they were going overland, that the battle was over; that their destination was another landing zone a few miles away;

that there they would be picked up and flown back to base camp, bringing this campaign to a close.

The young lieutenant questioned in his own mind why the move was on foot. Was this not the air cavalry? Did they not always move by helicopter? But he knew that he was just a lieutenant. He was not experienced like the sergeants and, at the lowest rank of the officers; his was not to question but to do.

The move was a difficult one. The jungle heat was oppressive, stifling the tired column of men, men loaded down with weapons and ammunition, completely soaked through with sweat. The men were also weary and disgruntled, clanging and cussing as they moved through the grasses and underbrush of this desolate highland terrain toward their destination.

The landscape changed as they moved; from the flat, openness of the embattled landing zone, up small hills, down shallow valleys bottomed by dry creek beds; then into highland jungle, thicker undergrowth made dark by tall trees, their tops growing together, forming a dark green canopy, choking off sunlight from the dimmed jungle floor.

The tired men continued their move; no words now, their silence dulled by exhaustion; only the occasional noise of their equipment breaking the stillness of the march.

The young lieutenant felt the same dullness, just one foot in front of the other, while his mind wandered; sometimes focused on the horrible scenes just left, sometimes thoughts of home, sometimes daydreaming, sometimes blank. Then, a stirring to the front. The column stopped. The captain on the radio, receiving information, receiving orders. "Move forward," came the command. "Through the rifle company to your front; something has happened."

The young lieutenant moved out with his men through chest-high bushes, then down and up another dry creek bed. Coming out of the sandy bed and into a small clearing, the young lieutenant saw his friend, his counterpart, the executive officer of the halted rifle company; his roommate in officer basic school, his roommate in paratrooper school, his cabin mate on the ship going over; sitting on a tree stump, steel helmet pushed back off his sweating brow.

"What the hell's going on, lieutenant?" his counterpart asked, his usual perky voice softened by the same exhaustion felt by all. "Pretty obvious, soldier," the young lieutenant shot back, a sly smile creeping across his face, showing the first sign of any emotion in hours; "They're calling the real fighting men forward."

The counterpart muttered an unpleasantry as the young lieutenant passed by, and laid a loud slap on the seat of the young lieutenant's trousers with the butt of an automatic weapon. A quick smile from both, one to the other, acknowledging the admiration, respect, friendship, that they each had for the other since the early days of officer training.

The young lieutenant now moved into a more open area as a radio operator informed him of the capture of two enemy soldiers by elements at the head of the column.

Emotions heightening now. Enemy in the jungle! But who were they? From what unit? Probably just stragglers from the previous three days' battle.

The column stopped again, spread out in a long line over hundreds of yards. The company commander and his radioman came past the lieutenant at a fast pace, moving forward on orders toward the activity to the front, leaving the young lieutenant and the rest of the company standing in place.

The column remained motionless, waiting for orders and curious about the events forward. A platoon sergeant, a soldier with combat experience, walked up to the young lieutenant; "What gives, sir? What's up?" The junior officer responded, "I don't know, sergeant; we're just stopped here while the brass sort things out."

"The men are tired, sir; can they rest?" the sergeant asked. "I guess so, sergeant; if they got 'em, let them smoke 'em." The men began dropping to the jungle floor, peeling off packs and weapons; steel pots hit the ground as cigarettes were lit and cans of cold rations opened and consumed.

The young lieutenant remained standing, observing, listening, with a strange feeling about this moment and this place. They were in no-man's-land, with enemy in the area; the company leaders and radio operators forward, the men drained by the move now resting on the ground, smoking, eating, dozing, with no hint of combat readiness.

And the place. The terrain was now flat and open, covered by tough elephant grass from knee to waist high, the ground punctuated by giant ant-hills; tall, hard clay mounds, about a man's height, rounded or pointed at the top, and tapering to a large base, large enough to lean against or hide behind. Rising straight up from the ground were high, strong trees with straight, limbless trunks, then spanning out into a dark green interlocking canopy high above the jungle floor.

The young lieutenant looked forward toward the front of the column where the officers had gathered and the two prisoners had been captured. To his left front, past numerous anthills and the trunks of tall trees, he could see an open area, brightened by a hot noon-day sun and large enough for several helicopters to land. *"The landing zone!"* he thought.

To the right of the stopped column and no more than a couple of hundred yards away was a thick, dark wall, an ominous barrier of trees, shrubs, and underbrush, which ran parallel to the column's direction of movement.

Then, time stopped.

Way off, from across the landing zone, past a clump of trees and past a second open area, came the muffled sound of a single shot from a weapon, followed immediately by a couple of more shots, then a quick burst from a distant automatic weapon.

The young lieutenant, surprised by the gunshots, and annoyed that someone failed to realize that the battle was over and that these men were waiting for helicopter pick-up, looked forward for an explanation.

Then all hell broke loose.

The dark green wall of undergrowth on the column's right flank erupted with the crack of small arms fire, the staccato of machine gun fire, the thump of mortar fire, and the explosion of hand grenades, shattering the stillness of the relaxed column of men with the unbelievable din of furious combat. The fire was interlocking, laying a sheet of deadly steel three to four feet above the ground, cutting down elephant grass, underbrush, and men, like a giant scythe reaping across the column's position.

The young lieutenant fell to the ground in the prone position, unlocking and pointing his automatic weapon in the direction of the unseen enemy, realizing that they had walked directly into an ambush but confused as to what to do.

Then he felt it.

The young lieutenant felt it for the first time. The most powerful emotion he had ever felt. He felt it reach its cold, steel claw right down his throat and grab his heart and soul and guts in an unrelenting grip so iron-clad tight that he was compromised. For the first time, the young lieutenant felt fear, the fear of combat, the fear of death; the fear that he had trained to overcome in Airborne School, in Ranger School, and had thought about a hundred times on the ship coming over and back at base camp; but he had no warning and no idea, no idea whatsoever that this fear would be so all-consuming, that its hold would be so paralyzing, so relentless, so unyielding.

Only moments ticked by before his training kicked in. The intensity of the battle escalated as the enemy rushed from its ambush position and closed with the surprised and debilitated column. The young lieutenant looked up through the elephant grass, saw a man in a khaki-colored uniform running toward an anthill near his own position; the young lieutenant aimed and squeezed, just like he had been taught, and the khaki-clad soldier fell. The young lieutenant dropped his face back into the dirt, elated that he had killed his first enemy, but pained that he had taken someone's son, husband, and father. He looked back in the direction from where he had just come; saw enemy soldiers too numerous to count overrunning the stalled American column; knew that his roommate's company, his buddy's company, had been all but annihilated; and the young lieutenant instinctively knew that his good friend whom he had just seen so alive only moments ago was down and probably dead.

Then a thought rushed into his brain, a thought that he wanted to avoid; that the captain was forward, away from the company, along with his radio operator, and that he, the young lieutenant, was in command of the ambushed company. The anxiety of being the leader, but with no orders or solutions, overtook him: "What should I do! What should I do!" he thought; "I am in charge, but I have no orders! I have no answers!"

Then, in a moment of weakness and indecisiveness, he reasoned, "I do not want to be in charge! I want someone else to lead! I don't know where anybody is! How can I do this!" This thought, only seconds in length, was interrupted by a sergeant, a squad leader, bleeding from a wound in his side, who crawled over and shook the young lieutenant and yelled above the furor of the battle sounds, "Lieutenant, what are we going to do? We are being butchered out here! We have got to do something!"

Then he knew.

The young lieutenant knew what to do. He had been trained for moments just like this. He was trained to assess the situation, make a decision, accomplish the mission, preserve his men. The mission and the men. The mission and the men. He knew he had to get his men out of the killing zone of the ambush.

The young lieutenant placed the butt of his weapon on the ground as he rose to survey the scene, moving above his sheltered, prone position, which was limited to only a few yards by the tall elephant grass. As he began his upward movement, the enemy machine gunner, tied high above in a tree and hidden by the green canopy of the intertwined tree tops, saw the lieutenant's ascension and sighted down on him as his next target of opportunity.

The first machine gun round hit the left side of the young lieutenant's helmet, penetrating and exiting the steel pot, grazing the lieutenant's left temple just above the ear, a stinging wound, blood flowing down into his olive drab shirt. The second round smashed into his left shoulder, shattering his collarbone near the joint and sending red hot, then white hot flashes of pain all through the left side of his body.

The young lieutenant fell backwards, slammed to the ground by the two hits, already screaming in pain, and absolutely amazed that someone had actually shot him.

He writhed on the jungle floor, gasping for breath, his heart beating furiously; his head up against the base of a tree. All of his feelings and fears now subordinate to the hurting he felt in his head and shoulder. The sergeant was back again. He crudely placed a bandage on the lieutenant's wounded shoulder and yelled again; "Sir, what do we do?"

Fighting through the agony and the shock of his wounds, the young lieutenant looked straight up the trunk of the tree, saw that its bark was flying from three sides, pointed his good right hand in the only direction that the tree was not receiving fire, and issued his only battlefield order: "Sergeant, move the men that way." "What about you, sir?" the sergeant screamed. "Just get the hell out of here, sergeant!" was the lieutenant's reply.

The sergeant and the men, at least those few who could, moved in the direction that the lieutenant ordered. The young lieutenant lay back in the tall grass, its sturdy blades wrapping around him, and strangely reminding him of the safety of his mother's arms. While tears welled in his eyes over the intense pain of his shoulder wound, he thought of his mother, of her tenderness, of her comfort, of her security, of her ability to make pain go away. Oh, how he needed her at this moment.

By now the enemy had overrun the column; as the young lieutenant lay motionless in the grass, he could feel the swish and movement as enemy soldiers raced by, yelling in their staccato, high-pitched voices and looking for wounded Americans to execute. He also felt the heat from the napalm, dropped by the friendly aircraft, almost on top of him; watched the grass around him wither and curl from the intense heat as the A-1E Skyraider pilots cooked the exposed enemy on the spot.

He knew he could remain no longer in this precarious position; he knew that he had no defense out here, that it would only be a matter of time; he knew that if the enemy did not finish him that his own men might. He knew he had to move.

Pushing up with his good right arm, the pain of his two wounds somewhat dulled now, he struggled to his knees to try and see a way out of this horrible place; a place now covered with the bodies of friendly and enemy, the hot earth soaked red with the blood of many good men; the stench of dust, gunpowder, and guts turning his stomach; his thoughts, senses, and feelings completely overcome by all that was around him.

The enemy machine gunner, still tied to his hidden perch in the trees above the young lieutenant's location, saw this last and final movement of the young officer, pointed the long barrel of the weapon at the center of the struggling man on the ground, and pulled the trigger.

Two rounds, fast and heavy, struck the young lieutenant flat in the chest, one just above the other, smashing and tearing almost every vital organ in a killing, mortal wound.

The powerful impact of the two large machine gun rounds knocked him brutally back to the ground with a force so terrible that he felt more numbness than pain. And he knew, he knew, that he was dying.

"Oh, Mama," he moaned, "Oh, Mama, you have lost your only son, you have lost your little boy. I'm so sorry, Mama. Please don't hurt too long for me, Mama. I'm so sorry, Mama. I'm so sorry."

The battle around him began to fade in his mind as his thoughts and feelings focused on his dying. His head began to swim; flashes of white, then red, racing through his brain as he began the long downward spiral towards death.

His body began to slow now, his life organs shutting down, unable to function in their fractured state. White hot thoughts, interrupted by jolts of pain, then the numbness of the tumbling spin of death. Drifting in and out of the reality of the moment; conscious, then not, his brain thinking, then fading, fighting for a last few moments of life; the white now red as the substance of him drained away.

Downward,

Downward,

The spiral,

His body falling dizzily through time and space. The red fading to purple, the purple darkening into black; no thoughts now, the blackness of the moment of death upon him.

And then, suddenly, amazingly, all stopped. The pain, the battle, the death spiral, all gone. His downward fall ceased. Reversed. Now being lifted upward with a movement so comforting, so unexplainable.

The young lieutenant was fully conscious and complete now, and bathed in a brilliant glow of white that he had never before experienced, encompassed in the invisible arms of a force more comforting than his own mother's embrace.

Then he heard a powerful voice that spoke directly to him, a voice with more authority than he had ever known, and yet with a calming tenderness greater than he could ever imagine, that brought him into a state of complete peace.

"Be still, young soldier;
Be still and know;
Your battle is over.
You have given all,
For your men,
For your army,
For your family
For your country.
You will hurt no more.
You have fought the good fight,
And you have won.
You have won
Because you are now with Me;
I have taken you out of that place,
That hell on earth,
To spend eternity with Me,
Where there are no guns,
No battles,
No enemy,
No wars,
No pain,
No death.
I am very proud of you, young lieutenant,
Very proud of you.
You deserve the eternal peace

Which now begins."
And the young lieutenant went to be with God.

Photo by Lt. Hank Dunn, the Artillery FO on LZ Albany—
Photo of LZ Albany area

Photo by Lt. Hank Dunn, the Artillery FO on LZ Albany

Photo by Lt. Hank Dunn, the Artillery FO on LZ Albany

The two NVA prisoners captured by members of the Recon Platoon, which was providing point on the movement into LZ Albany, before the ambush. Photo by Hank Dunn

Photo by Lt. Hank Dunn, the Artillery FO on LZ Albany

HISTORY REPEATED? AN OPINION

MUCH HAS BEEN MADE ABOUT the fact that we, the 2nd Battalion of the 7th Cavalry, almost repeated history on Landing Zone Albany on November 17, 1965. That we almost duplicated the history made by the 7th Cavalry in Montana on June 25, 1876. The key word here is "almost."

THE SIMILARITIES. First, Custer was outnumbered. Maybe ten to one. The 2nd of the 7th on LZ Albany was outnumbered, maybe six or seven to one. Second, Custer was surprised by the size of the Plains Indian encampment; 2/7 was surprised by the presence of the 8th Battalion, 66th Regiment, and the 1st and 3rd battalions of the 33rd Regiment of North Vietnamese regular soldiers. Third, Custer had limited intelligence; he did not know of the size and strength of the Indians. The 2/7 moving into Albany had limited intelligence; we had no idea that the North Vietnamese forces were camped there. And finally, Custer's 7th was annihilated on the banks of a river, the Little Big

Horn. The ambush on Albany occurred near a river, the Ia Drang ("ia" is the Vietnamese word for "river").

MISTAKES WERE MADE. Custer and General Terry divided his forces, sending Captain Benteen one way and Major Reno another. Nor was Custer properly supplied. And apparently Custer was egotistical enough to believe that he and his 7th Cavalry were invincible, and that the Indians could not possibly defeat him and his troopers.

In the Albany battle, we also made mistakes. We burned a storage hut on the way into Albany; the plume of smoke in the jungle announced our presence and location. Except for Delta Company's Recon Platoon, which was providing point, and Alpha Company, who were both moving in a tactical formation, much of the remainder of the column was in a more administrative attitude than a tactical one. And when the two North Vietnamese prisoners were captured by elements of the Recon Platoon, the column halted and basically took an administrative break. At least, that's how it felt back in the column. Why? Because we were told that we were moving to a landing zone to be picked up and flown back to base camp. And we were hot, tired, hungry, sleep-deprived, and had no orders to the contrary. We therefore assumed that the battle was over; that the 1st Battalion, 7th Cavalry had killed all the "bad guys" on X-Ray.

Finally, when the lead elements of the 2/7 reached the landing zone clearing, all the companies were "beheaded" when the company commanders and their radio operators were called forward, presumably for deployment around the LZ.

WHAT HAPPENED. On "Last Stand Hill," George Armstrong Custer and the men of Companies C, E, F, I, and L of the 7th Cavalry Regiment were completely wiped out by the superior force of Hostiles. On the other hand, things were different on LZ Albany. The initial phase of the battle favored the North Vietnamese. They had several major battlefield advantages—firepower, concealment, and, most importantly, the element of surprise. However, the battle turned. The soldiers of 2nd Battalion, 7th Cavalry rallied. They organized and established defensive perimeters. Alpha Company, the Recon Platoon from Delta Company, elements of the Command Group, and some stragglers from Delta Company organized and defended the front of the column from the copse of trees located between the two clearings that comprised the landing zone. Pockets of Americans from Delta, Charlie, and Headquarters companies organized and resisted back in the overrun column, and George Forrest's Alpha Company, 1st Battalion, 5th Cavalry did the same back at the rear of the column. The momentum shifted. The Americans went from "attacked" to "defender" to "attacker." And in the end, many more North Vietnamese died on that November afternoon than Americans. In fact, recent on-line North Vietnamese battlefield records have indicated that more North Vietnamese senior officers died on Albany than X-Ray, because everyone, from "cooks to colonels," rushed in to participate in the anticipated massacre of the Americans. By comparison, on LZ X-Ray, the 1st Battalion, 7th Cavalry had 79 American soldiers killed and another 121 wounded in two and one-half days of combat. On Albany, 155 American soldiers died and 124 were wounded in approximately eight hours.

THE DIFFERENCES. Pretty simple. Custer didn't have artillery support and two A1E Skyraiders overhead, armed with rockets, bombs, and napalm. And there were no "egos" on Albany; we did not have time for that. We were fighting to survive. I equate the American's situation on Albany with that of a boxer who has been knocked down and is being counted out by the referee. We were "down for the count." But we got up off the canvass, organized ourselves, found our resolve, and fought back. We were hurt, we were wounded, but in the end, we not only survived, but we prevailed. After dark, the North Vietnamese withdrew, probably back over the border into Cambodia, and changed their tactics in dealing with the Americans. It has been conjectured that the enemy took a new approach to fighting the Americans due to American fire and air superiority, but I truly believe that they also realized that the members of the United States Army could fight with tenacity when confronted. I think they felt that they had met their match.

MY CONCLUSION. The Battle on Landing Zone Albany was the single, most difficult experience I have ever suffered. It was a most horrific happening. To this day, I am haunted by the battle. Yet it had more to do with making me a man, making me a patriot, making me an American, than any other event in my life. And I am absolutely convinced that the American fighting man and the armed forces of the United States of America comprise the best fighting force in the world. I firmly believe that there is something inside us that makes us proud, patriotic, stubborn, resolved, and dedicated to defend freedom, to fight for that which is right and good, and to preserve the American way of life. Why do I believe that? Because I saw it.

ABOUT THE AUTHOR

JAMES TALBOT (JIM) LAWRENCE WAS born and raised in Troy, Alabama. He graduated from Troy High School in 1959 and The Citadel, The Military College of South Carolina, in 1963. He was commissioned a second lieutenant in March of 1964 and joined the 2nd Battalion, 9th Infantry, 2nd Infantry Division, stationed at Fort Benning, Georgia. He completed Paratrooper School and received his "jump wings" in the summer of 1964. When his 2nd Infantry Division unit was converted to the 1st Cavalry Division (Airmobile) along with the 11th Air Assault in the spring of 1965, Jim was named the 2nd Battalion, 7th Cavalry's first Reconnaissance Platoon Leader. Just weeks before the Ia Drang Valley campaign, Lawrence was promoted to first lieutenant and was named Executive Officer of Delta Company, 2nd Battalion, 7th Cavalry, the position he held during the battle at Landing Zone Albany on 17 November, 1965. For his service, Jim was awarded The Bronze Star, The Purple Heart, The Air Medal, The Army Commendation Medal, The Combat Infantryman's Badge, and other Vietnamese service medals. In 1967, then Alabama Governor George C. Wallace and the Alabama American Legion named him "the First Alabama Veteran of the Vietnam War."

After his military service was over, Jim taught English at Troy State University and the University of Alabama before pursuing a successful career in real estate in Birmingham, Alabama. He is married to Kathy, is the father to James Talbot Lawrence II, who is married to Jennifer Zeiler, who gave Jim and Kathy their first grandchild, Madelyn Grace Lawrence, born in April of 2012. Jim and Kathy live in Birmingham.

Jim Lawrence, Joe Galloway, Julia Moore, and General Hal Moore at a Veterans Day celebration in Decatur and Huntsville, Alabama

The author with Joe Galloway

Appendix

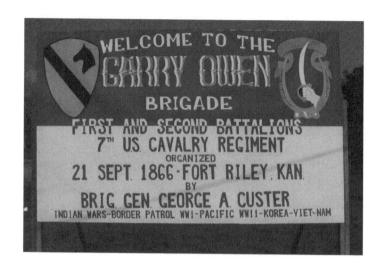

Garry Owen Brigade at An Khe

Front Row, L to R: Lt. Jim Lawrence, Lt. Oren Brown, CWO Ralph King, Lt. Mike Kalla.
Back Row, L to R: Capt. Myron Diduryk, Capt. "Skip" Fesmire, Capt. George Johnson, Capt. Charles McIntosh in front of An Khe Officers' Club

The 2/7 Officers Club, build after the Ia Drang with some "borrowed' material from the U.S. Navy at Qui Nhon harbor

Inside view of 2/7 Officers' Club

THE FOLLOWING ARE SONGS THAT were written and sung in the spring of 1966, several months after the Ia Drang campaign, by Major Frank Henry and lieutenants Larry Gwin, Rick Rescorla, Bud Alley, Jim Lawrence, and other lieutenants of the 2nd Battalion, 7th Cavalry, 1st Cavalry Division (Airmobile), with the able assistance of Budweiser, Schlitz, and Pabst Blue Ribbon, in the unit's "officer's club." The club was constructed primarily with materials "borrowed" from the United States Navy at Qui Nhon harbor during a "midnight reconnaissance."

The Men Of The Seventh

(To the tune of Ghost Riders in the Sky)
By Rescorla, Henry, Gwin, Alley, Lawrence, et al—1966

The men of Custer's Cavalry are fighting on today
They're fighting in a jungle of a land that's far away
No longer will the horses ever hear the bulges cry
The men of Custer's Cavalry are fighting in the sky.

CHORUS
Fighting, flying, Death may come tomorrow
Men who feel no fear or pain or sorrow
These are men who proudly claim to be
The Seventh Cavalry.

In Vietnam the Cavalry will answer freedom's call
The troopers of the sky will fight and many men will fall
But though they fell in battle I am sure that there will be
A special page in history for the Seventh Cavalry.

CHORUS

Now wars were fought and wars were won to keep our country free
And through them rode the horsemen of the Seventh Cavalry
They fought to keep their colors and their banners flying high
And now they fly their colors as the Horsemen in the Sky.

CHORUS

Come On Boys, Ride With Me

(By Rescorla, Henry, Gwin, Alley, Lawrence, et al—1966)

Come on boys and grab your sabers
Come on boys and ride with me
Give the cry of Garry Owen
Make your place in history.

One fine day in Ia Drang Valley
Came across the PAVN horde
Gave the cry of Garry Owen
Smote them with our bloody sword.

Ride away the battle's over
Many men have died today
Gave their lives for Garry Owen
Glory was their only pay.

Seventh went to Bong Son Valley
Came across the enemy
Once again, Garry Owen
Was the cry of victory.

Ride away the battle's over
Time to rest, we cannot stay
Saddle up with Garry Owen
Must return to old An Khe.

If the saddle fits your backside

And the saber fits your hand
Join the Seventh, Garry Owen
Gaining freedom for this land.

Jarheads landed to the north
With a mighty naval fleet
All they got was a lonely sniper
And a case of blistered feet.

So you're in the Special Forces
And you wear the Green Beret
Had you been with us in Ia Drang
You wouldn't be with us today.

So you think you're mighty Airborne
And you're drawing extra pay
Had you'd been with us in Crow's Foot
You wouldn't be with us today.

Think you're tough you Screaming Eagles
When you land at Cam Ranh Bay
Come and meet the real sky troopers
At their home in old An Khe.

If the saddle fits your backside
And the saber fits your hand
Join the Seventh, Garry Owen
Gaining freedom for this land.

VICTOR CHARLIE

(To the tune of Rock of Ages)

Author Unknown

Victor Charlie at Plei Me,
Threw a hand grenade at me
So I caught it in my palm,
Threw it back and he was gone
Victor Charlie at Plei Me,
Thanks a lot, you S.O.B.

THE LEGEND OF THE
SEVENTH CAVALRY

(SGT. FLYNN—The original words are of unknown origin,
but obviously written after the Battle of Little Big Horn.
The lyrics concerning the actions in Vietnam were added
by Lt. Rick Rescorla of the 2nd Battalion, 7th Cavalry, 1st
Cavalry Division (Airmobile) in early 1966.)

FIRST CHORUS
Garry Owen! Garry Owen! Garry Owen!
In the Valley of Montana all alone
There'll be better days to be for the Seventh Cavalry
When we charge again for dear old Garry Owen.

Once the Seventh rode with Custer, Sergeant Flynn
Against Sioux braves they did muster, Sergeant Flynn
Crazy Horse and Sitting Bull have got their bellies full
Of lead and steel from men of Garry Owen.

FIRST CHORUS

Though outnumbered and surrounded, Sergeant Flynn
Recall was not sounded, Sergeant Flynn
Men of Custer's cavalry you wrote our history
By death without dishonor, Garry Owen.

FIRST CHORUS

Now their bones have turned to dust, Sergeant Flynn
But they've left a sacred trust, Sergeant Flynn

From the annals of the brave comes a whisper from the grave
You have not heard the last of Garry Owen.

FIRST CHORUS

Now many years have passed, Sergeant Flynn
And the time has come at last, Sergeant Flynn
To Vietnam we go to fight a different foe
And join the fight for freedom, Garry Owen.

SECOND CHORUS
Garry Owen! Garry Owen! Garry Owen!
In the Valley of Ia Drang all alone
Better days have come to be for the Seventh Cavalry
And we'll charge again for dear old Garry Owen.

Here we stand in Ia Drang Valley, Sergeant Flynn
Round our guidons we must rally, Sergeant Flynn
Valiant men of history now show your gallantry
For the men who died with Custer, Garry Owen.

SECOND CHORUS

Through the night I hear them moving, Sergeant Flynn
I can hear their bugles playing, Sergeant Flynn
We're outnumbered I can see, but outfought we'll never be
For now bear the name of Garry Owen.

SECOND CHORUS

We are fighting at close quarters, Sergeant Flynn
Rifle, bayonet and mortars, Sergeant Flynn
We have given victory to the Seventh Cavalry
Let us charge once more for dear old Garry Owen

SECOND CHORUS

Now we proudly march away, Sergeant Flynn
For the Seventh won the day, Sergeant Flynn
Ghostly voices of the brave pay a tribute from the grave
We salute you, fighting men of Garry Owen.

SECOND CHORUS

GARRYOWEN

(The official song of the Seventh Cavalry, "Garryowen," was originally an Irish drinking song that was brought to America by Irish immigrants, some of whom served in the United State Army in the 1860's with George Armstrong Custer and the 7th Cavalry. Tradition has it that Captain Miles Keogh and other officers with ties to several Irish regiments in the British Army introduced the song to Custer, who liked it and adopted it because the beat of the song reminded him of the sound and rhythm of marching horses. The name came from a geographical landmark—a hill and a garden—near the city of Limerick, Ireland, which provided a view of the countryside and the Shannon River. The word, "Garryowen," is a compound of two words that translate "the garden of Owen." "Owen's Garden" is mentioned in other Irish literature)

(One of the original versions)
Let Baccus's sons be not dismayed,
But join with me each jovial blade,
Come booze and sing and lend your aid,
To help me with the chorus.

CHORUS
Instead of spa we'll drink dark ale
And pay the reckoning on the nail,
For debt no man shall go to jail,
From Garry Owen in glory.

We are the boys who take delight
In smashing Limerick lamps at night,
And through the streets like sportsters fight
Tearing all before us.

CHORUS

We'll break windows, we'll break doors,
The watch knock down by threes and fours,
Then let the doctors work their cures,
And tinker up our bruises.

CHORUS

We'll beat the bailiffs out of fun,
We'll make the mayor and sheriffs run,
We are the boys no man dare dun,
If he regards a whole skin.

CHORUS

Our hearts so stout have got us fame,
For soon 'tis known from whence we came,
Where're we go they dread the name
Of Garry Owen in glory!

GARRYOWEN
(7TH CAVALRY VERSION)

(Written by 7th Cav musician J. O. Brockenshire in 1905)

We are the pride of the army,
And a regiment of great renown,
Our name's on the pages of history,
From sixty-six on down.
If you think we stop or falter
While in the fray we're gin'
Just watch the steps with our heads erect,
While our band plays "Garryowen."

CHORUS
In the Fighting Seventh's the place for me
It's the cream of all the cavalry;
No other regiment ever can claim
Its pride, honor, glory and undying fame.

We know no fear when stern duty
Calls us far away from home,
Our country's flag shall safely o'er us wave,
No matter where we roam.
'Tis the gallant Seventh Cavalry
It matters not where we're goin'
Such you'll surely say as we march away;
And our band plays, "Garryowen."

CHORUS

Then hurrah for our brave commanders!
Who lead us into the fight.
We'll do or die in our country's cause,
And battle for the right.
And when the war is o'er,
And to our homes we're goin'
Just watch the step, with our heads erect,
When our band plays, "Garryowen."

CHORUS

FIDDLER'S GREEN

*(This poem, which was made into a song and sung by sol-
diers of the Seventh Cavalry, is of unknown origin. It first
appeared in a cavalry magazine in the 1920's. The poem
was altered after Custer's Last Stand, with the line "And put
your pistol to your head," added because it is said that some of
Custer's troopers saved a bullet for their own demise rather
than suffer capture and torture by the Indians. Even today,
when a cavalry trooper dies, he is said to be going to "Fiddler's Green," the fictitious stopover on the way to his next
eternal destination).*

Halfway down the trail to Hell,
In a shady meadow green
Are the Souls of all dead troopers camped,
Near a good old-time canteen.
And this eternal resting place
Is known as Fiddler's Green

Marching past, straight through to Hell
The Infantry are seen.
Accompanied by the Engineers,
Artillery and Marines,
For none but the shades of Cavalrymen
Dismount at Fiddler's Green.

Though some go curving down the trail
To seek a warmer scene.
No trooper ever gets to Hell
Ere he's emptied his canteen.
And so rides back to drink again

With friends at Fiddler's Green.

And so when man and horse go down
Beneath a saber keen,
Or in a roaring charge of fierce melee
You stop a bullet clean,
And the hostiles come to get your scalp,
Just empty your canteen,
And put your pistol to your head
And go to Fiddler's Green.

CPSIA information can be obtained at www.ICGtesting.com
Printed in the USA
LVOW01s1642181113

361724LV00002B/2/P